GOD Can Be Your Coach at Work

GOD

Can Be Your Coach at Work

*Inviting the Divine into Your Workplace to
Produce Success, Enjoyment, and Fulfillment*

By Wade Galt

Possibility Infinity Publishing

-

To GOD...

My Coach and Divine Inspiration.

To Dad...

My First Human Work Coach.

Ask and you shall receive.

Author's Note

In order for this book to be complete on its own, I have included some material from the first book, _GOD Can Be Your Coach_. This will allow those who have not read the first book to experience the benefits of this book without reading the first.

For those who have read the first book, you may enjoy re-reading these passages or you may choose to skip them if you prefer. I believe if you read all the chapters in order, you will receive the most benefit.

Whether you are reading for the first time or the fiftieth time, welcome! I hope you find this book insightful, enjoyable, practical, applicable to your daily life, and fulfilling.

Most of all, I hope you find whatever you have come here for. My intention is that this work helps you create a more powerful, loving, and purposeful connection with the divine, both inside and outside of work.

Create a great life.

Peace,

Wade

Notice

This book is about connecting with the divine and receiving divine wisdom. The author believes the knowledge and wisdom in this book are useful for anyone who seeks to enhance his or her connection with the divine. As with any discipline, results improve over time with consistent and focused practice.

The ideas and techniques presented in this book are not in any way intended to be a substitute for the advice of a physician or other licensed health care practitioner. If you are involved in psychotherapy, counseling or any other therapeutic relationship, it is advised that you not terminate treatment without consulting your therapist.

Any answer(s) or perceived guidance derived from the use of these methods should not be followed if it violates any local, state, federal or international law. Neither the author nor the publishers shall be liable or responsible to any person or entity for any loss or damage caused, or alleged to have been caused, directly or indirectly by the information or ideas contained, suggested, or referenced in this book.

It is the author's intention that this work leads the reader to a more powerful, personal, and practical relationship with the divine. The author believes the divine is the source of the answers he receives, and suggests that readers arrive at their own conclusions after using the techniques.

These Ideas Work For Me…

I wouldn't call them beliefs because I'm not attached to them. I'm not ready to kill or die to prove I'm right or that someone else is wrong. This is not dogma, so there's no need for anyone to argue. I'm not suggesting I'm right or others are wrong. I may be incorrect. I'm not saying I hold the only truth, the ultimate truth, or even truth.

This book is a collection of ideas that feel true to me, that inspire me, and that work for me (based on what I can see in my life). I'd love to hear how these and other ideas work for you. I see this as a two-way learning relationship that we can both learn from. I'm not the teacher. You're not the student. We're just two people exploring ideas about the divine in hope of improving our lives and the world.

Please Accept My Humility and My Grandiosity

It is my only intention that this work brings you closer to peace, love, joy, happiness, and a greater connection with the divine. Please excuse my limitations as a writer as I attempt to do this. It is not my intention to make anyone feel wrong, uncomfortable, that they need to change, or feel anything other than fully loved, accepted and supported.

Please accept my grandiosity in wanting to address such a huge and important subject (and any apparent presumption that I'm right). Please also accept my humility in doing my best to make myself vulnerable by sharing something I think will make the world a better place. I honor all those people, organizations, religions, beliefs, rituals, and everything else that seeks to do the same,

At the same time, I remain excited, open-hearted and open-minded to seeing how we may grow, evolve, and change how we relate with the divine and each other to bring about even more peace, love, and happiness.

Table of Contents

GOD Can Be Your Coach at Work

A year ago I co-wrote a book called *GOD Can Be Your Coach*. The book was all about how we can establish a powerful, personal and practical relationship with the divine. Writing this book was an amazing journey for me, and I really experienced the benefits of the book as I co-wrote it.

Today I find myself back at the computer typing for the same reason I went to the computer a year ago. I feel a bit lost. I don't feel as lost as I did a year ago, but I still feel like I'm missing something huge. Back then I felt confused about many things, and I desperately needed a stronger sense of direction and security. After all my other options failed, I turned to the divine and found more than I ever could have dreamed. I discovered and lived a life of peaceful surrender. I truly allowed myself to be guided by the most powerful being in the universe in the best way I knew how. As I opened up to divine guidance, I found myself feeling almost no stress. I felt very centered, purposeful, and fulfilled. I knew I needed nothing but the support of the divine, and I knew I already had that. Life was simple, peaceful and powerful. Other people noticed this and commented on how much more relaxed I was. Friends told me that for the first time in their life they saw me finally enjoying and savoring life, and they were right.

So what changed? Why am I back writing again? I had already intended to write this book, but I had "planned" to write it at a different time. I am finding that over the last few months, I've moved away from my connection with the divine. It appears that when I desperately needed the divine I was completely open to almost any and all guidance. I felt I had nothing to lose.

Recently, however, my business has taken off. Everything is going according to "plan." In fact, it's going even better. I'm making more money more quickly than I thought I would, and it appears there's even more to come. So what's wrong? I'm experiencing so much "success" right now that I can't get enough. I'm understanding very quickly what can happen in a business when growth happens quicker than planned. I feel a great need to re-simplify my life, just like I did last year, and bring my most important priorities into focus.

I can and will look to catch up on the latest and greatest business and leadership books, but I now remember something I had forgotten until a year ago. ***The divine is the greatest source of wisdom. If I can receive and follow divine wisdom, I will have all the direction and support I need.***

The best way to describe this is to use an analogy a coaching client I'm working with shared with me recently. We were discussing how he was experiencing an unbalance in his life because the overwhelming majority of his energies were going into his work. He was so focused on his work that he felt he was facing life alone. After we explored the situation deeper, he made a simple and extremely powerful statement to me. He said, "I've been living my life as if I'm an orphan, as if there's no God supporting me. I need to remember that I am a son (of the divine)."

Are you living your life as if you are an orphan?

Have you forgotten about your connection with the divine?

Are you opening up to receiving all the support that's available to you?

This book is about living your professional life with the fullest support from the most powerful and wise being in the universe. This is an opportunity to make God your coach at work. *

* If you prefer a different name for the source of all creation, then please substitute it for the word "God." A rose by any other name is still a rose. I do not believe the essence and the nature of the divine are changed by the names we choose.

Why Contact the Divine?

There is a part of us that is very wise, capable, centered, confident, secure, and able to do almost anything. There is also a part of us that is very unwise, incapable, scattered, scared, insecure, and *unable* to do almost anything. Most of us experience each of these ways of being at different times throughout the year, the month, the week, and the day. Few of us understand these shifts in our state of being, and even fewer of us have the ability to consciously and intentionally choose which state we wish to experience at a given time.

With all the insightful and brilliant self-help, self-image, positive thinking, and motivational books available, it would seem we have enough information to solve this challenge. The problem is *most self-help books fail to address one simple thing –*

there's only so much we can do as humans to help ourselves.

There is, however, no limit to what the divine can do to help us.

With the divine, anything is possible!

Experiential Exercises

This book contains a brief and powerful experiential exercise at the end of each chapter. These exercises are intended to help you to directly experience the words in this book. They, like this book, are simply one way of experiencing this material. They, like this book, are optional but recommended.

I encourage you to do these exercises as they are written the first time you read the book, and then customize them to best suit your needs. When you make them your own, they will become even more powerful for you.

At the end of the book, there is contact information for the author so you may share what you've done with the process and what you've experienced, if you like.

Enjoy... if you choose.

60-Second Experience #1

- ➢ **Set an intention to connect with the divine, and invite the divine to guide you in this process. ***
- ➢ **Open up to the possibility that you can connect with the divine.**
- ➢ Close your eyes and silently breathe in and out, focusing on your breath.
- ➢ Count to 3 as you breathe in, and count to 3 as you breathe out.
- ➢ Do this for 60 seconds (10 times in and 10 times out).
- ➢ **Notice how you feel.**
- ➢ Open your eyes.

* *An intention is simply a desire you wish to have fulfilled. Setting an intention to connect with the divine simply means declaring a desire to have the divine connect with you for this exercise. This declaration can be made silently within you.*

Why Would the Divine Guide Me?

If we focus on this question, we can find many reasons why we think the divine wouldn't help us. We have created many reasons why we think we will not be helped – *the divine doesn't care about us, other people are chosen to be guided but we're not, we're too stupid, too lazy, too bad, too selfish,* and so on. We can come up with a list of literally millions of reasons that all carry a similar theme – *"We're not good enough to be guided by the divine."*

Most of us have heard of the idea that we find what we are looking for in life. If we look for the negative and not so good things, we can find them. We can also find the positive and amazing things if we look for them. The question we need to ask ourselves is this…

Has thinking we are not good enough brought us closer to or farther from a powerful, practical, and personal relationship with the divine?

My answer is that it has brought me further away from the divine. When I told myself I wasn't worthy, I shut down and stopped communicating. This is no different than any other relationship I have been in. Whenever I thought I was dumber or less important than someone else, I did not feel comfortable speaking with them, and I stopped trying to relate with them. The same is true when I have thought someone was better looking, more popular, more fun, or in any way superior to me. I, like most people, simply did not feel comfortable relating with someone when I felt inferior in their presence.

Feeling inferior to someone can shut down our ability to relate with them. Notice this has nothing to do with what is actually true. The other person may actually be less smart than I am. The truth is not what disconnects me. My feeling of inferiority is what leads to the disconnection.

It is not necessary for me to feel superior to the person to connect with them. If I focus on something else, such as how much I enjoy communicating with this person, I can reopen to the possibility of connecting. Trying to make myself feel superior to someone else might only lead to them feeling inferior to me, which can also lead to their disconnection.

It's not important who is "better." In fact, if it is necessary for us to judge "better" and "worse", the "better" person would be powerful enough and open enough to connect with anyone without feeling their status or power is threatened. The smartest person in the world would not lose their intelligence by talking to the least intelligent. In fact, the smarter person may even experience joy from helping the less educated to become wiser. Many people know that helping another grow is one of the greatest joys in life.

If feeling inferior to the divine has kept you disconnected, it may be time to ask a different question, "Why wouldn't the divine guide me?" If the divine created me and sustains my life, and I humbly seek to receive guidance from the divine because I acknowledge I need the assistance, why wouldn't the divine help me?

This is not to say I'm looking to feel superior to the divine or that the divine owes it to me. I am not suggesting I'm entitled to divine guidance or that it will happen the way I want. I'm simply asking the divine to share with me the great wisdom that is available to the divine.

Maybe the divine does just what most of us do when a younger and less informed person asks us for guidance. Maybe the divine just gives when asked. Maybe the disconnection happens because of us and the way we think. Maybe the divine is simply waiting for us to connect and wanting to help us.

Of course, there is one significant challenge that is created once we acknowledge we can connect with the divine. "What are we going to do about it?"

Once we admit we can receive divine wisdom, we can no longer be victims. If we have the wisest being in the universe willing and available to guide us, we can't continue pretending we're helpless. Instead we are left with the wonderful invitation and challenge to move forward powerfully, lovingly, and divinely.

60- Second Experience #2

- ➢ Set an intention to connect with the divine, and invite the divine to guide you in this process.
- ➢ Close your eyes and silently breathe in and out, focusing on your breath.
- ➢ Count to 3 as you breathe in, and count to 3 as you breathe out.
- ➢ Do this for 30 seconds (5 times in and 5 times out).
- ➢ **Then declare (within you) that you wish to open up to receiving divine guidance.**
- ➢ **Ask the divine to help you feel worthy enough to receive divine assistance.**
- ➢ Breathe in and out for 30 more seconds.
- ➢ Notice how you feel.
- ➢ Open your eyes.

Does the Divine Care Abut Work?

Somewhere in human history we decided that the divine does not care about work. We told ourselves the divine was only concerned with "spiritual" matters and not concerned with "materialistic" things such as work. Though it may not be clear why we came to this conclusion, it is clear there are certain natural outcomes that have occurred in our world as a result of this belief.

Perhaps the most powerful everyday outcome of this belief is our pattern of having two different ethical codes – one for the working world and one outside of it. It has been said, "All is fair in love and war," but we have added "and work" as well.

Few of us fully live our highest spiritual values in our workplace. This is a common source of frustration, guilt, shame, and dissatisfaction for billions of us. We feel uncomfortable when we behave in ways that go against our highest values, but we unsuccessfully attempt to justify our actions by saying things like, *"I have to eat. It's a dog-eat-dog world, and I have to take care of my family. Business people are expected to stretch the truth to get the best deal; everybody knows that."*

And it's true. Everybody does know that. Virtually everyone who has been in the working world for more than a week knows there are situations where people will drop their ethical code to make money. The question is, "Does this really serve us to do so?" In the long run, does having a separate ethical code for work really help us? *If you have been living by two different codes, has it served you or hurt you?* Consider this before you read on.

If you're like most people, it may work for the quick fix, but it doesn't really do you justice over the long haul. Especially in the working world, most people agree that what goes around eventually comes around. If a person sows seeds of dishonesty, broken promises, and shady dealings, things will probably come back around in a way that leaves them worse off than before. Nature seems to compensate for imbalances automatically, even in the working world.

So why should a person risk living their spiritual values at work? Doesn't that put them in a handicapped position compared to others? Doesn't it leave them fewer options to address problems? It seems the simple answer is that *living by one ethical code is the easiest and most efficient thing to do.*

When we have all our energy moving in one direction towards a goal, we are most effective. *When we have to waste energy on things such as lying, remembering who we lied to, covering up lies, rationalizing why we lied, trying to keep our lies a secret, hidden agendas, feeling ashamed, feeling guilty, worrying about who will find out, and so on, we have very little energy left to do work.*

It just doesn't work as well. It's inefficient to be dishonest. It's like a liability on our Balance Sheet because at any time the truth can lead to significant loss. It's also like an expense on our Income Statement because we have to spend energy every month on covering up, hiding, emotional baggage, and other activities that rob us of our life, time, and money.

Whether or not we believe the divine will punish us for being dishonest, it's really not even relevant. When we're dishonest we punish ourselves.

The divine wants us to experience life, love, joy, fulfillment, abundance, and many other wonderful things. The divine cares about the working world because the divine cares about us. If we want help succeeding in the working would, we don't need to create a separate ethical code. We simply need to ask for help. *There is no question we can ask, no problem we can face that the divine is unable or unwilling to help us with.*

The decision to ask for help or not is up to us.

60-Second Experience #3

- ➤ Set an intention to connect with the divine, and invite the divine to guide you in this process.
- ➤ Close your eyes and silently breathe in and out, focusing on your breath.
- ➤ Count to 3 as you breathe in, and count to 3 as you breathe out.
- ➤ Do this for 30 seconds (5 times in and 5 times out).
- ➤ **Then declare (within you) that you wish to live by one divinely inspired ethical code.**
- ➤ **Ask the divine to help you do find the strength, understanding, and confidence necessary to do this.**
- ➤ **Be still, listen and receive any guidance that comes to you.**
- ➤ Breathe in and out for 30 more seconds.
- ➤ Notice how you feel.
- ➤ Open your eyes.

Is It Wrong to Ask the Divine to Help Me with Financial and Work Issues?

Rather than tell you what I believe about this, I invite you to engage in a question and answer process. Simply answer the questions in order. If you have any difficulty answering any of the questions or if you feel confused, I invite you to simply close your eyes, get centered, ask the divine for assistance, and see what comes to you.

1) Who or what is the wisest force in the universe?

2) Who or what gave you life?

3) Does this being care about your well being?

4) Would this being help you if you asked?

5) Would this being help you address a problem or situation that affected your spiritual life?

6) Would this being help you address a problem or situation that affected your personal life?

7) Does your work life affect your personal life and spiritual life?

8) Do your personal life and spiritual life affect your work life?

9) Is there any good reason why this being would not help you address a problem or a situation in your work life?

10) When are you going to begin asking for help?

60-Second Experience #4

- ➤ Set an intention to connect with the divine, and invite the divine to guide you in this process.
- ➤ Close your eyes and silently breathe in and out, focusing on your breath.
- ➤ Count to 3 as you breathe in, and count to 3 as you breathe out.
- ➤ Do this for 30 seconds (5 times in and 5 times out).
- ➤ **Then declare (within you) that you wish to be guided by the divine in your work life.**
- ➤ **Ask the divine to help you do this in a way that the divine supports.**
- ➤ Be still, listen and receive any guidance that comes to you.
- ➤ Breathe in and out for 30 more seconds.
- ➤ Notice how you feel.
- ➤ **Thank the divine.**
- ➤ Open your eyes.

What is a Coach?

A coach is anyone who inspires you to be a better you. A coach helps you create the world you most desire, achieve your most important goals, and be the person you most wish to be.

People have been coaching other people in the working world for as long as people have been doing business; however, the term "coaching" has only recently become popular. Most consultants, mentors, managers, leaders, supervisors, executives, and people with all other types of titles have played the role of coach at some point in their relationships with their co-workers. A good coach supports and challenges the coachee at the same time. A good coach balances supporting the coachee when outside help is needed and challenging the coachee when the coachee has the ability to help him or herself.

The best coaches simultaneously accept their coachees exactly as they are and invite their coachees to become an even higher version of who they most wish to be.

Good coaches can accept their coachees as they are because they see the perfection in the unfulfilled goal. They can see that the first grade child is simply a perfect, but younger, version of the future twelfth grade adolescent. Good coaches enjoy the process of self-creation, and they love watching and helping others become who they most wish to be.

Good coaches love their coachees, love themselves, and they love growth. They love the processes of self-definition, self-discovery and self-mastery. They feel privileged to be part of someone else's evolutionary process. They accept, appreciate, enjoy, admire, challenge, inspire and love their coachees at every step of the process.

Simply put, *good coaches love their coachees towards growth.*

God is the best coach of all.

60-Second Experience #5

- ➢ Set an intention to connect with the divine, and invite the divine to guide you in this process.
- ➢ Close your eyes and silently breathe in and out, focusing on your breath.
- ➢ Count to 3 as you breathe in, and count to 3 as you breathe out.
- ➢ Do this for 30 seconds (5 times in and 5 times out).
- ➢ **Declare that you wish to be inspired by your life and by this process.**
- ➢ **Ask the divine to help you do this.**
- ➢ Be still, listen and receive any guidance that comes to you.
- ➢ Breathe in and out for 30 more seconds.
- ➢ Notice how you feel.
- ➢ Thank the divine.
- ➢ Open your eyes.

The Qualities of a Great Coach

Not all people in leadership or supervisory positions act like coaches. Many people with power act like dictators, manipulators, and a variety of other roles that are not focused on inspiring the coachee to do his or her best. Such people may only be concerned with getting the most out of their employees, without concern for the employees' well being and growth.

Coaching is different from other roles in many areas. Below are some of the most critical areas.

1) A great coach's power lies in their being (who they are), not their role.

2) Great coaches hold themselves accountable first.

3) Great coaches meet their own needs first.

4) Great coaches need nothing from their coachees.

5) Great coaches have no personal agenda for their coachees.

6) Great coaches facilitate development with questions rather than answers.

7) Great coaches will not accept their coachee's power, even if the coachee tries to give it away.

8) Great coaches will not accept their coachee's responsibility, even if the coachee tries to give it away.

9) Great coaches help hold coachees accountable to themselves, not the coach.

10) Great coaches evoke action through the coachee's inspiration rather than coach's motivation.

1) A great coach's power lies in their being (their person) not their role.

Great coaches are powerful people who might or might not have powerful positions. They don't spend time reminding you what their job title or position is because that is not where their power lies. They constantly demonstrate their power by the person they are and the actions they take. All the coachee needs to do is follow their powerful example.

2) Great coaches hold themselves accountable first.

Great coaches have the power to hold themselves accountable to themselves. This power is the foundation of their ability to help others hold themselves accountable. Without this power, significant positive change and growth happens rarely or slowly since most life-changing insights and plans are not acted upon. With this power, consistent grow occurs regularly, and anything is possible.

3) Great coaches meet their own needs first.

Great coaches meet their needs from within. They take care of themselves so well that they do not need to lean on others to get their needs met. Whatever needs they can't meet for themselves, they get met outside of their relationship with their coachees. (Usually, they get coached themselves).

4) Great coaches need nothing from their coachees.

Because they can meet their own needs, great coaches need nothing from their coachees. They do not need approval, attention or anything else that might cause them to put their own needs before the needs of the coachee.

5) Great coaches have no personal agenda for their coachees.

Because they need nothing from their coachees, great coaches have no personal agenda for their coachees. They do not need the coachee to validate their ability as a coach by reaching a certain goal or particular outcome. Unlike some parents who live their lives through the successes and failures of their children, a coach's value as a coach is not determined by the performance of the coachee. Great coaches are free to focus all their energy on helping the coachee attain the coachee's goals because energy is not being spent on trying to meet their own needs and goals.

6) Great coaches facilitate development with questions rather than answers.

Great coaches do not have anything to prove. Their purpose is to ask questions that help the coachee get to the desired answer. If the coachee asks a question the coachee can answer for himself or herself, a great coach will redirect the coachee by inviting them to find the answer for him or herself. If the coach has a unique area of expertise, the coach will share what they know in a brief manner.

7) Great coaches will not take accept the coachee's power, even if the coachee tries to give it away.

Great coaches are extremely aware of where their power lies (within) and where their coachee's power lies (within the coachee). Great coaches encourage their coachees to accept their power, and all interactions with the coachee facilitate this empowering process. Even if the coachee tries to give their power to the coach, the coach will not accept it. They will, instead, invite the coachee to reclaim it.

8) Great coaches will not accept their coachee's responsibility, even if the coachee tries to give it away.

Great coaches are equally aware of where their responsibility lies (within) and where their coachee's responsibility lies (within the coachee). Great coaches lead their coachees to accept their responsibility. If the coachee tries to give their responsibility away, the coach will not accept it. They will, instead, invite the coachee to reclaim it.

9) Great coaches help hold coachees accountable to themselves, not the coach.

Since a great coach has no personal agenda for the coachee, the only person to hold the coachee accountable is himself or herself. The coach may facilitate this accountability with powerful questions that lead coachees to examine how well they are holding themselves accountable to their own agendas, but the ultimate accountability lies with the coachee. Great coaches may ask the questions, but only the coachee will answer them.

10) Great coaches evoke action through the coachee's inspiration rather than the coach's motivation.

Motivation is an external driver; inspiration is an internal force. Most people are motivated to pay their bills (because they have to or they will face a consequence from an external source). Great coaches are inspired to help their coachees because they love to (from a desire within). Great coaches arouse that same energy in the coachee. They help the coachee find an inspiring vision to energize the coachee's body, heart, mind, and spirit. They know if a person is energized on all four of these levels (physically, emotionally, mentally, and spiritually), the person will have all the power, drive, and energy they need. They will not need outside sources (such as fear of failure, fear of loss of approval, or anything else) to take them to their desired outcome.

The divine is the greatest coach of all. The divine meets and exceeds these qualities better than any other being. The divine is everything and needs nothing. The divine is the only being who can always be fully present to supporting us because the divine has no unmet needs.

Human coaches are good. The divine is perfect.

60-Second Experience #6

- ➢ Set an intention to connect with the divine, and invite the divine to guide you in this process.
- ➢ Close your eyes and silently breathe in and out.
- ➢ Do this for 30 seconds.
- ➢ **Invite the divine to be the main guiding force in your life.**
- ➢ Be still, listen and receive any guidance that comes to you.
- ➢ Breathe in and out for 30 more seconds.
- ➢ **Make a commitment to do what you need to do and be who you need to be in order to live the wisdom you receive.**
- ➢ Thank the divine.
- ➢ Open your eyes.

Getting Coached By the Divine

There are an infinite number of ways to connect with the divine. Below is a one way that you might structure a coaching session with the divine.

1) *Awareness* – Bring to mind all the things, blessings, and people in your life you are thankful for. Be open to seeing all the ways the divine has already blessed you in your life. Notice what you love about your life, and express your gratitude if you like.

2) *Intend Connection* – Create an intention to connect with the divine and align your actions, feelings, thoughts, and commitments with the divine so you might better serve yourself and others.

3) *Connect in Silence* – Be still, forget what you think you know, and quiet your mind. Breathe in and out slowly and gently. Feel the presence of the divine as you breathe.

4) *Declare* – Declare what you wish to be, do or have.

5) *Ask* – Ask the divine to support you in understanding how to make that happen.

6) *Receive* – Be still and listen to your inner wisdom (that still, small voice within) to get your answers.

7) *Specific Action* – Ask for a specific way that you can direct your actions, feelings, thoughts and commitments towards the outcome you seek.

8) **Commit** – Decide to act upon the insight you receive and abandon ALL excuses.

9) **Gratitude** – Thank the divine again for all the guidance, insight, wisdom, life and support you receive.

The entire process takes as little as 1 or 2 minutes. If it is supported by your actions, feelings, thoughts, and commitments, you can change your life forever.

You may use the process as often or as seldom as you like. Like exercising, the benefits you receive usually reflect how often you use this process and how well you implement the wisdom you receive.

Here is an example of how I am using the process right now.

1) **Awareness** – *"God, thank you for all the amazingly wonderful blessings in my life. I am amazingly blessed and truly grateful for everything I have and everything I am. Thank you for life."*

2) **Intend Connection** – *"My intention is to connect with you and with divine truth. Please guide me in your ways and truths."*

3) **Connect in Silence** – I took 5 deep breaths in and out and said (internally) to the divine, "Please Guide Me" with each breath until I was still.

4) **Declare** – *"I wish to make others aware of this book and this work in a way that honors and demonstrates the principles in this book."*

5) **Ask** – *"How can I help get this work to those who would most benefit for it?"*

6) **Receive** – I received the following message from inside – *"First, know without a shadow of a doubt that those who are supposed to receive this work will do so in their time. Knowing this, simply write the work and make all those around you aware of it."*

7) **Specific Action** – I then asked, *"How should I do this?"* and my inner wisdom told me, *"Place information about it on your website, tell your friends, email your clients, and take out ads in magazines that reach people interested in work and spirituality. Attempt to convince no one. Simply make people aware of the work. Know that it will get to those who will benefit from it. Come back for more guidance or details any time you need. For now, simply write the book."*

8) **Commit** – I committed to doing this and wrote the above words.

9) **Gratitude** – I then thanked the divine for the guidance, wisdom, and support I received. Then I received the message, *"You receive because you ask. You are welcome to receive anytime you wish."*

60-Second Experience #7

- ➤ **Bring to mind everything and everyone in your life you are thankful for.**
- ➤ **Notice all the ways the divine has already blessed you.**
- ➤ Set an intention to connect with the divine, and invite the divine to guide you in this process.
- ➤ Close your eyes and silently breathe in and out.
- ➤ Do this for 30 seconds.
- ➤ **Declare that you wish to receive all of the benefits available from connecting with the divine.**
- ➤ **Ask the divine to help you become comfortable communicating with the divine through this process.**
- ➤ Be still, listen and receive any guidance that comes to you.
- ➤ Breathe in and out for 30 more seconds.
- ➤ **Ask the divine to show you specifically how you can make this desire come true.**
- ➤ Make a commitment to do what you need to do and be who you need to be in order to live the wisdom you receive.
- ➤ Thank the divine, and open your eyes.

Does This Really Work?

There is only one simple way to know the answer to this question, and that is to experience a connection with the divine. We could say the only way to know if it works or not is to "try", but then we find ourselves back in a familiar place of having our outcomes determined by our beliefs.

Saying we wish to "try" something is quite different from declaring we intend to experience something. *When we state we are coming from a place of trying, it's as if we have already said, "I'm really not sure this thing is going to work, but I guess there's nothing to lose, so I'll give it a shot."*

If I had to bet my money on an athlete who felt this way about playing in a championship game, I would feel better giving my money to charity. At least I know I'd get something out of my money. (I would guess this athlete had about a 20% chance of succeeding and an 80% chance of losing).

We "try" because we're afraid to fail. We're afraid to declare to the world that we're going to do something and then find out that we are unable. We're even more terrified about the possibility of the world discovering that we're unable. When say we'll try, we make an excuse before we even begin. Imagine a doctor operating on you for you who says, "I really didn't have a good childhood, and I didn't have the best training, but I'll *try* to fix your broken leg."

Intending an experience is a whole different matter. Just listen to the difference in the language:

- I'll try to see if I can do this.

- I intend to do this.

Intending is far more powerful than trying because it confidently declares a purpose and an anticipation of success. There is nothing wishy-washy about it. A person who intends is clear about what they wish to create or experience, and they have confidence in their ability to do it. *Clear intention with decisive action is very powerful.*

Even if they have no more experience or talent than another person who is trying, a person who is intending is already far more prepared for success. They are confidently expecting to make something good happen and ready to take an active role in creating their success, while the other ("trying") person is doubtfully hoping something will happen to them. A person who tries passively hopes things will work out. They have little or no confidence, a weak plan or no plan at all, and are not ready to take powerful action.

If the self-fulfilling prophecy holds true, the person who tries will usually experience failure, occasionally experience success, and almost never actively influence the outcome. The person who intends will experience success more often than not (or at least more often than the person trying), occasionally experience failure (and for such a person "failure" is simply the process of learning what does not lead to success and then doing something else), and they will always play an active role on influencing the outcome in their favor.

Simple equations for each may look like this…

Trying =

60% **Doubt** + 30% **Hope** + 5% **Plan** + 5% **Action**

All of this equals **90% Uncertainty** (Doubt and Hope) and **10% Directed Action** (Plan and Action). The person has 10% going for them, thus a maximum guaranteed success rate of 10%.

Even if this person's hope works for them half of the time, that's just another 15% (1/2 of 30%) added to the success rate. So the hopeful person has an average success rate of 25%.

The intending equation looks like this…

Intending =

25% **Clear Vision** of Desired (Positive) Outcome +

25% **Anticipation** of Desired (Positive) Outcome +

25% **Plan to Achieve** Desired (Positive) Outcome +

25% **Action** to Achieve Desired (Positive) Outcome

All of this equals 100% of energy going in the direction of success. The maximum guaranteed success rate = 100%. Even if this person has a faulty plan and takes incorrect action half of the time, there's still a 75% average success rate. (They only lose 25% from 1/2 of the 50%).

Now here's the simple answer to the question, "Does this really work?" *This really works if you intend it to.*

If you have…

1) **A Clear Vision of the Desired Outcome** (receiving guidance from the divine that helps you lead a more fulfilling life) <u>PLUS</u>

2) **Anticipation of the Desired Outcome** (anticipating that the divine will help you if you're open to receiving guidance) <u>PLUS</u>

3) **A Plan to Achieve the Desired Outcome** (using the ideas in this book or some other plan that you feel confident will work for you) <u>PLUS</u>

4) **You take Bold Action to Achieve the Desired Outcome** (confidently and powerfully taking the actions you have chosen),

…then it is very likely you will create or experience what you most desire. Even if you do not experience success immediately, you will persist until you do. *This is what's called unbending intention – an intention that remains strong and does not change until it is fulfilled.* No outside forces stop it. This is the type of intention that the most powerful people on the planet demonstrate in their lives. They decide (intend) to create something powerful, and they will do whatever it takes for however long it takes until they succeed.

You can have unbending intention if you wish. You can be a powerful co-creator with the divine. You can experience divine connection if you wish. The only question left is, "Are you going to intend to connect with the divine or are you going to try?"

The answer to that question is the same as the answer to the question, "Does this really work?"

60-Second Experience #8

- ➢ Bring to mind everything and everyone in your life you are thankful for.
- ➢ Notice all the ways the divine has already blessed you.
- ➢ Set an intention to connect with the divine, and invite the divine to guide you in this process.
- ➢ Close your eyes and silently breathe in and out.
- ➢ Do this for 30 seconds.
- ➢ **Declare that you wish to shift from a person who tries to a person who intends.**
- ➢ **Ask the divine to help you become comfortable with powerfully intending the grandest vision of what you most desire.**
- ➢ Be still, listen and receive any guidance that comes to you.
- ➢ Breathe in and out for 30 more seconds.
- ➢ Ask the divine to show you specifically how you can make this desire come true.
- ➢ Make a commitment to do what you need to do and be who you need to be in order to live the wisdom you receive.
- ➢ Thank the divine, and open your eyes.

How Do I Know I'm Connected?

There is no guaranteed way to prove a person is connected with the divine, but there are many ways of knowing for yourself. When we are connected with the divine, we feel many divine-like feelings at the same time.

Some of the many divine-like feelings we experience include:

Peace	*Calmness*	*Joy*
Compassion	*Acceptance*	*Freedom*
Centeredness	*Knowingness*	*Bliss*
Abundance	*Affluence*	*Creativity*
Wisdom	*Timelessness*	*Purpose*
Unconditional Love	*Oneness with the Universe*	

These are just some of the feelings we may experience when we connect with the divine. We may also feel certain sensations in parts of our body that let us know we are connected. Some people feel a sense of love in their heart, while others might feel a tingling sensation in their head. Other might feel sensations throughout their entire body.

The more you connect with the divine, the more you'll become familiar with how it feels for you when you are connected. This will allow you to become better at knowing when you are receiving guidance from your spiritual mind, as opposed to your emotional (feeling) or intellectual (thinking) minds.

60-Second Experience #9

- ➢ Bring to mind everything and everyone in your life you are thankful for.
- ➢ Notice all the ways the divine has already blessed you.
- ➢ Set an intention to connect with the divine, and invite the divine to guide you in this process.
- ➢ Close your eyes and silently breathe in and out.
- ➢ Do this for 30 seconds.
- ➢ **Declare to the divine that you wish to always be aware of when you are connected and when you are not.**
- ➢ **Ask the divine to help you know when you are not connected so you may take the opportunity to re-connect.**
- ➢ Be still, listen and receive any guidance that comes to you.
- ➢ Breathe in and out for 30 more seconds.
- ➢ Ask the divine to show you specifically how you can make this desire come true.
- ➢ Make a commitment to do what you need to do and be who you need to be in order to live the wisdom you receive.
- ➢ Thank the divine, and open your eyes.

Are You Feeling Connected or Disconnected?

As you read the following words, really internalize them and experience them. Remember the times you have felt this way.

When we're not aware of our connection with the divine we can feel disconnected, alone, insecure, afraid, judged, uncomfortable, edgy and other similar constrictive feelings. We engage in our addictions in an attempt to escape our feelings and our reality. If we could just get away for a little while, we'd feel so much better. But we can't. We're trapped in our own private hell as we walk around the earth. Nothing seems to be working right for us, and everything seems to be stacked against us. It's as if the world is conspiring to bring us down. We argue with our friends, our loved ones and our co-workers. Nobody wants to be around us and we feel so lonely. The news just confirms how horrible the world is, and we know that tomorrow isn't going to be any better. We feel anxious and worried about every little detail of life. We are afraid about what might happen tomorrow, and we beat ourselves up over what happened yesterday. We stay up at night worrying and spend the day obsessing. Life appears able to only produce misery. Life is miserable.

After reading about feeling completely disconnected from the divine, how do you feel?

Are you relaxed or short of breath?

Is your heart beating slowly or quickly?

Are you feeling calm or anxious?

Do you feel comfortable or uncomfortable?

Do you feel empowered or disempowered?

Think about your grandest goal...do you think you can do it?

Think about your greatest fear...does it concern you more or less than usual?

How close do you feel to the divine?

Now, as you read these words, really internalize them and experience them. Remember the times you have felt this way.

When we are completely aware of our connection with the divine, everything feels great. We feel relaxed, comfortable, safe, confident, loved, secure, supported, accepted, and a variety of other positive and expansive feelings. These feelings lead us to take action powerfully and confidently. We are strong when the divine is working through us, and we feel a sense of purpose and meaning that we lack otherwise. Everything seems to be working for us, and we feel like an athlete who's "in the zone." The universe is conspiring to help us and support us in all we do. We know we can't fail, so we succeed. Our confidence is so contagious that we positively impact all those around us. People are drawn to us and want to spend time with us. Abundance naturally beats a path to our door, and we feel at one with everything and everyone. We can let go of anything because we know the divine is always there to guide us and provide for us. We live fully in the present moment because we're not feeling sorry about the past or worrying about the future. We sleep well at night, and we wake up full of energy. Life is full of wonder. It's wonderful.

After reading about feeling fully connected with the divine, how do you feel?

Are you relaxed or short of breath?

Is your heart beating slowly or quickly?

Are you feeling calm or anxious?

Do you feel comfortable or uncomfortable?

Do you feel empowered or disempowered?

Think about your grandest goal...do you think you can do it?

Think about your greatest fear...does it concern you more or less than usual?

How close do you feel to the divine?

Feeling connected or disconnected with the divine can make all the difference in the world. It can determine whether or not we have the confidence, energy, and focus to achieve our greatest goals or repeat our biggest failures. The outcome often depends on whether or not our state of being promotes or prevents our success.

Opportunity + Our State of Being = Outcome

If we spend the majority of our time disconnected, we reduce the odds that we will be successful because our state of being may prevent it. If, however, we are usually connected, our opportunities will usually be converted into successes.

We all have opportunities. The most successful, fulfilled, and happy people make the most of all of their opportunities. It may be true that some people appear to have more opportunities than others, but that means nothing if the opportunities are not maximized.

Staying connected with the divine maximizes our chances of taking advantage of all the wonderful opportunities that come our way. When we do this, life is full of meaning, abundance, success and fun.

60-Second Experience #10

- ➢ Bring to mind everything and everyone in your life you are thankful for.
- ➢ Notice all the ways the divine has already blessed you.
- ➢ Set an intention to connect with the divine, and invite the divine to guide you in this process.
- ➢ Close your eyes and silently breathe in and out.
- ➢ Do this for 30 seconds.
- ➢ **Ask the divine to help you know when you are not connected by allowing you to feel some feeling in your body or some other clear and obvious sign.**
- ➢ **Declare that you will go inside and reconnect for 5 seconds whenever you feel this feeling.**
- ➢ Be still, listen and receive any guidance that comes to you.
- ➢ Breathe in and out for 30 more seconds.
- ➢ Ask the divine to show you specifically how you can make this desire come true.
- ➢ Make a commitment to do what you need to do and be who you need to be in order to live the wisdom you receive.
- ➢ Thank the divine, and open your eyes.

Bringing the Divine with You to Work

If you were a computer programmer, and you could bring the best programmer in the world to work with you every day (at no charge) to advise you how to best do your work, would you?

If you were a talk show host, and you could bring the best host in the world to work with you every day (at no charge) to advise you how to best interview people and attract great guests, would you?

If you were an investor, and you could bring the best investor in the world to work with you every day (at no charge) to advise you how to best invest your clients' money, would you?

Do you think the divine is as knowledgeable as any of the best people in these fields of work?

Do you think, perhaps, the divine is more knowledgeable than the best people?

Do you think the divine knows better than any other being how to help you to best do your work?

If you could bring the divine to work with you every day (at no charge) to advise you how to best do your work, would you?

If you've answered, "yes" to the last question, and you're not bringing the divine with you to work, what's stopping you?

60-Second Experience #11

- ➢ Bring to mind everything and everyone in your life you are thankful for.
- ➢ Notice all the ways the divine has already blessed you.
- ➢ Set an intention to connect with the divine, and invite the divine to guide you in this process.
- ➢ Close your eyes and silently breathe in and out.
- ➢ Do this for 30 seconds.
- ➢ **Declare that you wish to seek divine guidance whenever you have questions about your work or your life**
- ➢ **Ask the divine to help you to always be aware of the times when it would serve you to receive divine guidance.**
- ➢ Be still, listen and receive any guidance that comes to you.
- ➢ Breathe in and out for 30 more seconds.
- ➢ Ask the divine to show you specifically how you can make this desire come true.
- ➢ Make a commitment to do what you need to do and be who you need to be in order to live the wisdom you receive.
- ➢ Thank the divine, and open your eyes.

Regular Coaching with the Divine

You may find you wish to engage in a formal or structured coaching relationship with the divine. You may decide to choose a regular time to connect and even address certain items with the divine. There is no magic formula to this, though there are many powerful ways to do this. Depending on your style, you may use a variety of tools at different times. Below are some ideas of how to do this.

Regular (Scheduled) Times, Loose Structure

A very powerful way of connecting with the divine is to schedule a regular time when you connect to receive guidance. This allows you to create deep connections because your body and mind get used to, and eventually anticipate, the time you spend connecting. You may decide to connect for a short amount of time daily or you may decide to commit to long periods of time on a weekly basis. Experiment to find out which works best for you.

Regular Structured Times

Another powerful way involves connecting in a formal or structured coaching relationship. You may decide to have a specific process or progression of 10 to 30 minute sessions that repeats every 3 months or so. An example may look something like this…

Week 1   Establish Connection and Express Gratitude for All My Blessings

Week 2	Share My Goals with the Divine and Ask for Clarity About Which Ones Will Best Serve Me
Week 3	Ask for Clarity About How to Measure Success with Goal(s) and Set Target Dates for Goal(s) Completion
Week 4	Define Specific Action Steps for Completion of Your Goal(s)
Weeks 5-10	Ask for Weekly Action Step(s) to Help You Reach Your Goal(s)
Week 11	Ask for Clarity about Any Loose Ends
Week 12	Express Gratitude for Divine Help

Daily Connections

Some people prefer to live their life from their divinity rather than humanity. This usually implies living from their divine wisdom rather than their brain or intellect. If we use our brain to guide our life, we will find ourselves limited by the capacity of the brain. We will probably structure our lives based on traditional and conventional thought because those are the types of thoughts our brain produces. (Just like a computer, *our brain gives back to us what we put into it, but it does not generate new ideas*).

Divine wisdom, on the other hand, is the source of our inspirations and creative leaps. *When we tap into divine wisdom, we go beyond the limitations of our pre-programmed thoughts and learned thinking.* We access the guidance that can tell us precisely what's best for us in each moment. This guidance is not limited by the boundaries of human thought.

A person may receive the guidance to work on Mondays from 7-3, Tuesdays from 10-4, go fishing on Wednesday mornings to rejuvenate and work from 2-5, work on Thursdays from 8-6, and Fridays from 10-2. Maybe this is the schedule that would lead to optimum performance, creativity, and success for this person. Maybe this seemingly unconventional schedule would be exactly what this person needs to make their next creative leap. Maybe our conventional thoughts about working a structured workweek that lasts for a certain number of hours every day isn't the most effective thing. *Maybe the divine knows something we don't.*

As we get more comfortable connecting, we may find ourselves looking for guidance daily. We may realize we don't need to plan everything out three years, three months or even three weeks in advance. We may decide to simply connect every morning for 5 minutes and receive guidance from the divine about what would be best for us to do next. *It may seem scary for us to let go of our plans and schedules and trust another to guide our life. It may not seem so scary, however, when we realize it is the divine we are trusting our life with.*

Question and Answer Sessions

Receiving guidance from the divine can be a very informal matter. You may simply decide to ask the divine for guidance on various questions you have. You may also choose to write down questions that come up for you during the week and then ask for guidance in a single daily or weekly sitting (or "coaching session"). This is a very simple way of connecting with the divine that can fit in easily with your current schedule and way of living.

Immediate Connections

You may decide to connect with the divine anytime you have a question. Anytime you need assistance, you might take a few moments or minutes and get the guidance you need right away. If the question is not urgent and you would prefer to connect later, you might simply wait until a better time presents itself later in the day. This may be the easiest way of connecting to remember. ***Whenever you feel unsure or don't know, simply ask the divine.***

Constant Connection

Some people stay aware of the divine at all times. Instead of waiting for a question or crisis to come up, they proactively maintain as constant of a connection with the divine as they can. This way, they are most prepared for questions or potential crises that await them. Since they are so prepared, very few things actually become a crisis for them. They only have situations they must respond to. For these people, not being connected is the exception to the rule. The overwhelming majority of the time they are ready for anything that comes their way.

The greatest spiritual teachers and role models share this quality. This is why they are so wise and ready to respond to situations. They spend their time bathing in the wisdom and guidance of the divine rather than simply calling on the divine when a problem occurs. They may appear to others to be the source of their power, centeredness, and wisdom, but they know the truth and tell those who ask that their true source is the divine.

There are no "shoulds" when it comes to connecting with the divine. There is only whatever works best for you. It is probably best for you to experience personally and decide which way or ways helps you in the way you most wish to be assisted. (In order to fully inform yourself of what is the most powerful way for you, you may want to try each of the suggested ways, as well as any others you come up with).

The most important thing to know is that you can ALWAYS connect whenever you want. Truly and fully knowing that you have access to the guidance and support of the most powerful being in the universe any time you want completely eliminates all stress, anxiety, and worry. All of it! The times when we feel stressed, powerless, and lost is when we forget (or when we don't completely know) what type of support and guidance is available to us by simply asking.

60-Second Experience #12

- ➢ Bring to mind everything and everyone in your life you are thankful for.
- ➢ Notice all the ways the divine has already blessed you.
- ➢ Set an intention to connect with the divine, and invite the divine to guide you in this process.
- ➢ Close your eyes and silently breathe in and out.
- ➢ Do this for 30 seconds.
- ➢ **Declare that you wish to connect with the divine in whatever way or ways that are most powerful for you.**
- ➢ **Ask the divine to help you do this and to help you KNOW COMPLETELY that you can connect with the divine at any time.**
- ➢ Be still, listen and receive any guidance that comes to you.
- ➢ Breathe in and out for 30 more seconds.
- ➢ Make a commitment to do what you need to do and be who you need to be in order to live the wisdom you receive.
- ➢ Thank the divine.
- ➢ Open your eyes.

Your Personal and Professional Mission

One of the most basic questions of all time for humans to answer has been, "What's my purpose?" We long to know why we are on the Earth and what we are here to do or be. The interesting thing is that even though many (possibly most) people are still looking to answer this question for themselves, there seem to be plenty of people ready to tell us what they think we should be or do. Some of the people who may have very strong and definite opinions about our lives include our friends, family, co-workers, the media, society, religious institutions, and other organizations. *Since many of these same people seem to have not yet found their own mission, it appears the best answers will come from our creator.*

Many people believe a mission or purpose in life must be tied to a specific job or vocation. Such people appear to believe it is only possible to live out their mission if they engage in a certain type of work. This may explain why so many of us feel like we're not doing what we're called to do. Feelings like this can lead to frustration, disappointment, and even despair. It can feel like the reason we don't feel fulfilled in our work is that we haven't found what we need to be doing.

From this viewpoint, we associate fulfillment with doing. We're really saying this...

If we do activity A, then we will be fulfilled.

If we don't do activity A, we won't be fulfilled.

We are saying that our beingness (being fulfilled) depends on our doingness (doing activity A). If this is true, then we can only be fulfilled when we are active. We would have to constantly do in order to be fulfilled. If we were not doing, we would not be fulfilled.

There are a few inconsistencies in this logic. First, many of us experience being fulfilled when we are simply enjoying a moment with a friend, watching a loved one or being still in nature. In each of these examples, we are not really doing anything.

Second, as has been pointed out by many writers before, if our beingness depends on our doingness, then when we stopped doing we would stop being. Clearly this is not the case.

Third, there are many ways to do any job. A person can take a job as a social worker or a nurse (jobs that most people consider as meaningful and helpful) and do the job in a way that is disrespectful, unloving and harmful to the people they work with. Similarly, a person cake take a job as a financial planner or salesperson (jobs considered by many to be either self-serving or primarily financially-oriented), and that person can do the job in a way that is respectful, loving and totally in tune with meeting their clients' needs. In each of these examples, it is the person's beingness that determines how they do the job, not the other way around. *It is possible for a person to be fulfilled in many types of work if he or she does the work in a way true to his or her beingness. A loving person doing work in a loving way will almost certainly experience fulfillment.*

It may be more accurate to say there are certain types of work where we *feel* more fulfilled or have more fun. This does not change the fact that we can *be* fulfilled in various types of work if our beingness is focused on doing work in a fulfilling way (whatever type of work it is). We may choose to reword our earlier statement to read like this…

If we do activity A, then we will <u>feel</u> fulfilled.
If we don't do activity A, we won't <u>feel</u> fulfilled.

As we mature, we may find we can be *and feel* fulfilled in almost any type of work. Then we can see that we are the ones who are responsible for bringing our fulfilled beingness to our work. Knowing this can be very helpful during times when we have to do work or specific tasks we don't really like – something that happens in all types of jobs. We can still be fulfilled while we do our paperwork, even if we prefer meeting with clients, and we can experience fulfillment in all the work we do.

A simple way of doing this is for us to stay mindful of why we do what we do. Many people keep items in front of them to remind them what's most important to them. If we look to experience fulfillment by helping the poor, and we work at a place that doesn't focus on this purpose, we may keep a picture in front of us to remind us of our mission. A picture of our family can help us remember why we work and we can connect with the feeling of fulfillment that comes from knowing we're supporting those whom we love most.

Of course, we may choose to find the work we enjoy most and bring our fulfilled beingness to that work. In this way, we set ourselves up for success by finding the work that is most enjoyable to us (our favorite doingness) and bring our fulfilled self (beingness) to it. In doing this, we demonstrate our recognition that *the fulfillment is in us, not the work. We don't look for the fulfillment in the work because we know it's not there. We look for fulfillment where it's always been – within.*

60-Second Experience #13

- ➢ Bring to mind everything and everyone in your life you are thankful for.
- ➢ Notice all the ways the divine has already blessed you.
- ➢ Set an intention to connect with the divine, and invite the divine to guide you in this process.
- ➢ If you like, close your eyes.
- ➢ Silently breathe in and out for 30 seconds.
- ➢ **Declare to the divine that you wish to bring your fulfilled beingness to your work.**
- ➢ **Ask the divine to help you know how to best do enjoyable work in a fulfilling way.**
- ➢ Be still, listen and receive any guidance that comes to you.
- ➢ Breathe in and out for 30 more seconds.
- ➢ Ask the divine to show you specifically how you can make this desire come true.
- ➢ Make a commitment to do what you need to do and be who you need to be in order to live the wisdom you receive.
- ➢ Thank the divine.
- ➢ Open your eyes.

Turning Your Mission Into an Inspiring Vision

If you want to know how likely it is that you will actually act on your life mission, examine how inspiring your life vision is.

If you have created a crystal clear picture in your mind that excites you, energizes you, pumps you up emotionally, fills you with love, gets your creative juices flowing, keeps you up at night pondering possibilities, and makes you really want to get up out of bed early in the morning, then you have a very good chance that you will act out your mission and succeed in fulfilling your vision.

On the other hand, if you have a fuzzy idea of what you want, and thinking about your vision or your work makes you feel confused, tired, insecure, uncertain, lazy, bored, or other similar feelings, you probably will not act out your mission or succeed in fulfilling your vision. In fact, you may not even want to get out of bed. You might just decide to call in sick for this life.

An inspiring vision is so critical because it helps generate the energy and excitement necessary for you to want to happily work towards the realization of your goals and dreams. Your overflowing excitement naturally leads you to take powerful actions. You become interested in learning what you need to know, meeting whom you need to meet, and doing what you need to do. What you don't know, you find out. You can do all of this for one simple reason – you have an abundance of energy available to you.

Your energy is the fuel for the journey towards fulfilling your vision. We all have similar vehicles (our bodies), but without the necessary fuel (energy and excitement) the fastest car in the world will go nowhere. Do you get that? *It doesn't matter how intelligent, powerful, strong, good-looking, popular, or friendly you are. Without fuel, there is no motion.*

So a good guide for you is to see how emotionally excited you become when creating your vision. *If you are not excited by your vision, you still need to work on it.* It may just need to be fine tuned rather than overhauled, but it still needs work. If there's no spark, there will be no fire.

This is true for all dimensions of your life. If the vision or the idea of having children doesn't inspire you, how excited are you going to be to change the diapers and get up in the middle of the night? If the vision of doing a certain type of work bores you to death, know that it will literally bore you to death. (It will literally suck your energy daily until you slowly die). If the vision of marrying a certain person makes you miserable, know you will be miserable. (And he or she will probably be, too).

Your energy about a vision simply gives you an idea of what lies ahead. If you feel great about it and can see good things, then you've taken the right first step. There will be many other steps to fulfilling your vision, but your high energy level will be a huge factor in setting you up for success. If you don't feel great about your vision, then you still have work to do. After all, *if you set a boring goal, and you hit it, the best that can happen is that you end up bored.*

While excitement is a necessary quality for fulfilling a vision, it is not enough by itself. It is possible to be excited by a vision and still have very little chance of attaining it. Below are some of the reasons excitement alone may not be enough:

- Believing the vision is not possible.
- Inability to overcome others' beliefs that the vision is not possible.
- Lack of willingness or discipline to take the necessary actions.
- Lack of willingness to ask for help when it's needed.
- Expecting the divine or someone else to do all the work for you.
- Lack of confidence to take powerful action.

Whatever the reason, it is certain *the divine can give us the guidance, confidence, support, or whatever else we may need to fulfill our highest and boldest vision(s). All we need to do is ask and we will receive all the help and guidance we need.*

60-Second Experience #14

- ➢ Bring to mind everything and everyone in your life you are thankful for.
- ➢ Notice all the ways the divine has already blessed you.
- ➢ Set an intention to connect with the divine, and invite the divine to guide you in this process.
- ➢ If you like, close your eyes.
- ➢ Silently breathe in and out for 30 seconds.
- ➢ **Declare to the divine that you wish to receive a vision of your work that will inspire you.**
- ➢ **Ask the divine to help you let go of any doubts you may have and open up what is possible when you connect with the divine.**
- ➢ Be still, listen and receive any guidance that comes to you.
- ➢ Breathe in and out for 30 more seconds.
- ➢ Ask the divine to show you specifically how you can make this desire come true.
- ➢ Make a commitment to do what you need to do and be who you need to be in order to live the wisdom you receive.
- ➢ Thank the divine and open your eyes.

Living Your Life's Purpose at Work

There is no magic formula for living your life's purpose at work, but there are questions that will help you get clearer about what it looks like. Take some time to answer the following questions for yourself. Write down the answers on a sheet of paper as they come to you. It will serve you to first take a few moments to connect with the divine.

Vision

1. How may I live my life's purpose in a way that serves others and nourishes myself?

2. What special qualities or divine gifts do I possess that will help me live my life's purpose in a way that serves others and nourishes myself?

3. How may I best maximize these divine gifts in a way that serves others and nourishes myself?

4. What human qualities do I possess that will make it difficult for me to live my life's purpose in a way that serves others and nourishes myself?

5. How may I best manage these special human qualities in a way that serves others and nourishes myself?

6. How might I best serve others in a way that serves me and the fulfillment of my life purpose?

Details

7. What, specifically, would it look like for me to live my life purpose at work?

8. How would I spend my time?

9. What activities would I need to do?

10. What would I need to read or learn about?

11. What type of people would I need to meet, receive support from, and work with?

12. What can I do right now to experience being fulfilled?

13. How will I know for sure that I'm living my life's purpose at work? (What signs will tell me?)

60-Second Experience #15

- ➢ Bring to mind everything and everyone in your life you are thankful for.
- ➢ Notice all the ways the divine has already blessed you.
- ➢ Set an intention to connect with the divine, and invite the divine to guide you in this process.
- ➢ If you like, close your eyes.
- ➢ Silently breathe in and out for 30 seconds.
- ➢ **Declare to the divine that you wish to live your divine life purpose at work.**
- ➢ **Ask the divine what you can do today to help you begin doing this.**
- ➢ Be still, listen and receive any guidance that comes to you.
- ➢ Breathe in and out for 30 more seconds.
- ➢ Ask the divine to show you specifically how you can make this desire come true.
- ➢ Make a commitment to do what you need to do and be who you need to be in order to live the wisdom you receive.
- ➢ Thank the divine and open your eyes.

Making Your Work Sacred

There is no type of job that is guaranteed to be "spiritual" or "divine." A job title does not automatically make a job (or the person doing the job) divinely inspired. Doing work in a divinely guided way and being a person who connects with the divine to enhance their work makes work sacred.

Many of us have spent a large part of our lives looking for the "right" job that will make us feel "spiritual" or "good". We may decide we want to help homeless people, protect animals, heal the sick, feed the poor, clothe the naked, and many other similar things.

While all of these activities are powerful and may be very spiritual, there are a few key points to note about them if we wish to keep ourselves from idealistically (and inaccurately) romanticizing them.

1) *"Sacred" work can be done in both sacred and not-so-scared ways.*

2) *"Ordinary" work can become sacred when the fruits of the work (i.e. money and other compensation) are used to support "sacred" purposes.*

3) *"Sacred" can mean a variety of things, depending on whom you talk to and how you view the world.*

Most of us have heard of people who have taken on very "sacred" job roles and acted in not-so-sacred ways. We can do work in a way that is loving, kind and supporting of others and ourselves.

We can also do work in ways that are only self-serving, harmful to others, and everything but loving. We can do work both ways no matter who we work for.

Work that seems ordinary can become extraordinary when it is used to support causes we consider sacred. A person may not feel their work is sacred, but they may use their money to support charities, feed their family, educate their children, heal themselves, and many other similar activities.

Any time we call work "ordinary" just because we don't see the sacredness in it, we run the risk of oversimplifying things. If a person works for a non-profit agency and uses all their money for themselves without feeding their children, are they more or less sacred than a person who works as a bartender and gives all their money to charity?

When we start trying to evaluate these things, we risk becoming judgmental and "playing God." The truth is, we simply don't have all the information available to us that the divine does. *We may be best served by letting the divine make such judgments, if in fact the divine chooses to do so.*

Similarly, it may be best for us to understand that our definition of "sacred" may be very different than someone else's. Again, it may serve us to simply live our own life and let the divine relate with each of us individually. Besides, it appears we each have been given enough to work on with the divine (on ourselves) for our lifetime. We really don't need the additional responsibility of trying to fix someone else.

60-Second Experience #16

- ➤ Bring to mind everything and everyone in your life you are thankful for.
- ➤ Notice all the ways the divine has already blessed you.
- ➤ Set an intention to connect with the divine, and invite the divine to guide you in this process.
- ➤ If you like, close your eyes.
- ➤ Silently breathe in and out for 30 seconds.
- ➤ **Declare to the divine that you wish to bring a sense of sacredness to your work.**
- ➤ **Ask the divine to help you know the best way that you can do this.**
- ➤ Be still, listen and receive any guidance that comes to you.
- ➤ Breathe in and out for 30 more seconds.
- ➤ Ask the divine to show you specifically how you can make this desire come true.
- ➤ Make a commitment to do what you need to do and be who you need to be in order to live the wisdom you receive.
- ➤ Thank the divine and open your eyes.

Changing the World with Your Work

Despite what most people think, the world's "problems" are very simple to fix. They are not complex at all. They are, however, very difficult to fix because of the levels we usually operate on as a world. We usually operate primarily from either desperation or motivation.

When we operate from desperation, we are only concerned with our own needs because we feel so powerless we can't even imagine being able to help someone else. We operate primarily from our physical and emotional dimensions. We feel like we're not enough, like we won't make it, or we aren't loved, and we search for the answers only in the physical world. We focus on meeting our basic physical needs, and we shut off our intellectual and spiritual dimensions. We can't think clearly because we're so emotionally powerless and confused, and we don't contact the divine because we feel hurt, abandoned, unloved, undeserving, and alone.

When we operate from motivation, we are so concerned with our own needs (because we feel so powerless without our possessions, achievements, and other such external sources of validation and power) that we can't even imagine being able to share them with someone else.

When we are grounded in the motivation mindset, we operate primarily from our physical, emotional, and intellectual dimensions. We think if we know enough and acquire enough, we will make it, we will be loved, and we will find the answers we seek in the physical world. We focus on satisfying all our richest physical desires, and we shut off our spiritual dimension. We don't contact the divine because we believe happiness is to be found primarily or only in the physical world. We may feel guilty about the abundance we have or scared that connecting with the divine will make us feel sorry for "all those desperate people" and give away the possessions we crave so addictively.

In both of these ways of being, *the spiritual dimension is avoided because people are perceived as separate from us and the physical world is seen as a limited source for the fulfillment of our needs. We believe there simply isn't enough to go around for everyone, so we either become scared or paralyzed and take no action to help ourselves or we become obsessively self-focused or possessive and only take action to help ourselves.*

If we open up to inspiration, we will find the divine has all the answers and abundance we seek. We will also find that we have all the answers and abundance we seek if we can just learn to share. *We can end world hunger tomorrow by simply redistributing the food on the planet.* We can stop crime tomorrow by simply choosing not to violate one another. We can stop hate tomorrow by simply taking responsibility for our own problems rather than blaming them on others.

All of these ideas appear to be completely irrational. They seem to appeal to faith rather than human reason. Actually, this is not correct. Just because we do not understand how these ideas would work, it does not mean they are irrational. Galileo's inspired discovery that the Earth revolves around the Sun was thought to break the rules of human reason and knowledge, so he was called "irrational." It was soon discovered that he was not breaking the rules of human reason and knowledge. He was expanding them. He was transcending (going beyond) human reason. His inspirational discovery, when compared to human reason, was trans-rational (beyond reason).

As is common, his inspired break with contemporary human reason caused a great deal of commotion, yet now we accept his findings as fact.

When we tap into inspiration, we open up to divine wisdom and understanding. We let go of our boundaries and blocks to seeing what's possible. When we are inspired, we accurately feel that anything is possible. We are not being delusional. *When we are inspired by the divine, we accurately perceive the simple truth that has been written about and professed for thousands of years – with the divine, all things are possible. ALL THINGS!*

When you bring the energy of inspiration to your work and to those you touch, you begin the transformation of the world – one person at a time.

60-Second Experience #17

➢ Bring to mind everything and everyone in your life you are thankful for.

➢ Notice all the ways the divine has already blessed you.

➢ Set an intention to connect with the divine, and invite the divine to guide you in this process.

➢ If you like, close your eyes.

➢ Silently breathe in and out for 30 seconds.

➢ **Declare to the divine that you wish to be divinely inspired and inspire all the people you meet.**

➢ **Ask the divine to help you know the best way that you can do this.**

➢ Be still, listen and receive any guidance that comes to you.

➢ Breathe in and out for 30 more seconds.

➢ Ask the divine to show you specifically how you can make this desire come true.

➢ Make a commitment to do what you need to do and be who you need to be in order to live the wisdom you receive.

➢ Thank the divine and open your eyes.

Bringing Divine Energy to Work

We can choose to bring our awareness of the divine into our workplace. We can ask for guidance to help us work in a way that is in alignment with our highest and most divine self. We can choose to bring meaning and divine purpose to our work even if the work, by itself, doesn't seem very spiritual.

We can ask the divine to help us see how we can bring divine qualities and energies into our workplace, and we can be people who interact with others from a place of divine connection. We may also ask for divine guidance as to how we may proceed with business decisions, how to create the most beneficial business outcome for all parties involved in a transaction, and any other guidance that can help us bring our divine aspect into our work. *There's no greater source of wisdom, on any topic, than the divine. When we align our work with the divine, we set ourselves up for success, enjoyment and fulfillment.*

We can do all this without upsetting others. We don't have to tell anyone of our divine connection, and we don't have to make others wrong for not using their connection. When others see the peace, enjoyment, fulfillment and success we experience, they will naturally come to us wanting to know how we're doing what we're doing and being who we're being – or maybe they won't. It really doesn't matter. If we're content with the quality of our connection with the divine and the way we're living our lives, other people's opinions will matter very little.

If we really use our divine connection at work, we can experience something amazing. *We can live our divine purpose in our work and get paid for doing it. We won't have to wait until we're outside of work to make a positive difference in the world.*

We don't need to join a non-profit or charitable organization to make our impact on the world, and we don't need to travel to a foreign country. When we align with the divine, we can make the world a better place right where we are. After all, where else is there?

60-Second Experience #18 *

> ➢ Bring to mind everything and everyone in your life you are thankful for.

> ➢ Notice all the ways the divine has already blessed you.

> ➢ Set an intention to connect with the divine, and invite the divine to guide you in this process.

> ➢ Close your eyes and silently breathe in and out.

> ➢ Do this for 30 seconds.

> ➢ **Declare that you wish to be divinely inspired in the workplace.**

> ➢ **Ask the divine to help you use your work to move towards your goals, dreams and divine life purpose.**

> ➢ Be still, listen and receive any guidance that comes to you.

> ➢ Breathe in and out for 30 more seconds.

> ➢ Ask the divine to show you specifically how you can make this desire come true.

> ➢ Make a commitment to do what you need to do and be who you need to be in order to live the wisdom you receive.

> ➢ Thank the divine, and open your eyes.

* This exercise is a great way to stay connected with the divine while you're at work. It can be extremely helpful to do this exercise every hour or so. Not only will it give you the spiritual benefits of feeling connected with the divine. It will also help you relax physically, quiet your mind and helps settle your emotions. This exercise, as with all the others, can quickly bring a sense of peace and other divine qualities to your world and to your being.

Working with the Divine and Others

With the divine as our coach, it might seem we would never have any need to go to any other being for help. This is true; however, it appears there is a need for humans to relate with each other and to experience the outside physical world.

Though there is no human being who knows more than the divine, interacting with others to receive information allows us to form relationships with fellow human beings. It allows us to experience communication with each other and the co-creation process. Together we can experience connection, teamwork, a sense of belonging, inspiration, unity, and many other similar things. When we work together in such a way, we feel the power that comes from working together to reach a goal or fulfill a purpose. Such an experience of unity, though it may not provide any more information than interacting directly with the divine, provides us with a divine-like experience of connecting powerfully with something bigger than ourselves. We experience the power of collective purpose and cooperation. At times like these our lives are enriched with an even broader range of experiences. We get to experience deep connection with each other AND with the divine. Just like when we connect directly with the divine, we feel whole, powerful, centered, and alive. It is truly a joy to experience such unity.

There are times, however, when group interactions do not go so smoothly. We may find ourselves arguing with others, finding fault with others, or simply unable to be open to other points of view. At times like these, it can feel like the divine is nowhere to be found. We may tell ourselves how right we are and how wrong the other person or people are. We may defend ourselves because we feel attacked or rejected by the other. At times like these, our connections may feel everything but divine.

At such times, it will serve us to reconnect with the divine. We may decide to take a break from the group to re-center ourselves. It may serve us to literally leave the area where the group is and find a quiet place to reestablish our connection. While connecting, we can ask the divine for guidance as to how we may re-enter the group in a fresh, centered, powerful, and loving way. In this way we begin the process of working together harmoniously again.

This cycle of the group working together then getting stuck might (and probably will) happen many times. The simple nature of people is to desire closeness then space, then closeness, then space. When we know this, we can more easily step back from the group without taking things personally, knowing there will be a time for the group to be close again.

Of course, if each member of the group also practices connecting with the divine, it will be even easier for everyone to co-manage the ebb and flow of the group. If everyone is able to connect with the divine for guidance, the group will operate powerfully when it is together and when it takes time apart. Such groups are truly powerful as they offer us a chance to interact with each other in a divinely human way. *Rather than simply talking about living divinely, we get to practice this way of being with each other and experience the amazingly powerful transformations that result from shared divine connection.*

60-Second Experience #19

- ➢ Bring to mind everything and everyone in your life you are thankful for.
- ➢ Notice all the ways the divine has already blessed you.
- ➢ Set an intention to connect with the divine, and invite the divine to guide you in this process.
- ➢ Close your eyes and silently breathe in and out.
- ➢ Do this for 30 seconds.
- ➢ **Declare that you wish to interact with others in ways that inspire them to connect with their divinity.**
- ➢ **Ask the divine to help you do this.**
- ➢ Be still, listen and receive any guidance that comes to you.
- ➢ Breathe in and out for 30 more seconds.
- ➢ Make a commitment to do what you need to do and be who you need to be in order to live the wisdom you receive.
- ➢ Thank the divine and open your eyes.

Connecting with Your Eyes Open

Eventually, you'll be able to connect very quickly and very strongly. *You can also reach a point where you can connect to the divine with your eyes wide open. As you do this, your life and your work will become a living meditation. You can live your highest spiritual values in every moment you stay connected.*

The more time you spend connected, the closer you get to living from your spiritual (divine) mind – just like the greatest spiritual teachers. Each moment you spend connected; you get closer and closer to continually living a life that reflects divine qualities:

Peace	*Calmness*	*Joy*
Compassion	*Acceptance*	*Freedom*
Centeredness	*Knowingness*	*Bliss*
Abundance	*Affluence*	*Creativity*
Wisdom	*Timelessness*	*Purpose*
Unconditional Love	*Oneness with the Universe*	

This is enlightenment. This is purposeful living. This is what a life-transforming relationship with the divine is all about.

60-Second Experience #20 *

➢ Bring to mind everything and everyone in your life you are thankful for.

➢ Notice all the ways the divine has already blessed you.

➢ Set an intention to connect with the divine, and invite the divine to guide you in this process.

➢ **Keep your eyes OPEN and silently breathe in and out for 30 seconds.**

➢ Focus on your breath and count to 3 as you breathe in, and count to 3 as you breathe out.

➢ **Declare to the divine that you wish to be connected every moment you are awake.**

➢ **Ask the divine to help you maintain your connection at all times.**

➢ Be still, listen and receive any guidance that comes to you.

➢ Breathe in and out for 30 more seconds.

➢ Ask the divine to show you specifically how you can make this desire come true.

➢ Make a commitment to do what you need to do and be who you need to be in order to live the wisdom you receive.

➢ Thank the divine.

** If you do this exercise enough, you may reach a point where you can stay connected to the divine at all times simply by breathing in the way you breathe when you're doing these exercises. Your awareness of your breathing will be a reminder of your constant connection with the divine. As you breathe purposefully, you will **consciously** bring the divine into your life in **every** moment.*

Staying Connected

If you could maintain a constant connection with the most powerful and wise force in the universe, would you? The answer seems so obvious, yet for most of us, our actions say "no." Perhaps this difference between our intention to be connected and our actual actions relates to our ideas of what it means to be connected.

There are many ways of being connected to the divine. We don't have to be in any particular form of worship, prayer, meditation or any other practice to connect with the divine. We simply need to ask and to be aware. We might decide to simply take a few deep breaths and think of the divine for 5 seconds. We might close our eyes and silently express gratitude for our life and all our blessings or we might say a favorite prayer that reminds us of our connection with the divine.

One way of remembering is to wear something to remind you of your connection with the divine. If you wear a special ring or piece of jewelry, you might become aware of your connection with the divine each time you see it or feel it. The item doesn't need to be expensive or flashy. It simply needs to remind you.

Another way to remind yourself is to have items present in your home or place of work that remind you of your connection. These items can be anything from a beautiful picture of the ocean to items of religious or spiritual importance that help increase, amplify, or express your connection with the divine.

Another way is using noises as reminders. If you have a watch or clock that makes sounds on a regular basis, you might remember your connection with the divine anytime it makes a noise. This could be every hour, every 15 minutes or ay other amount of time. It simply depends on how often we wish to be reminded of our connection. *Every time we connect, our lives get better. Connect all the time, and only the divine knows how wonderful our lives can be.*

When we connect with the divine, we feel centered, calm, powerful, loving, kind, generous, abundant, and many other wonderful things. As we spend more time connected, we spend more of our life in the state of being we most desire. This state of being helps us to be more creative, effective, loving, confident and successful – which leads us to feel even better about ourselves and the divine.

There is no limit to how often we can connect with the divine – other than always. We don't have to stop what we're doing. When we're working we can remember to be thankful for our job, and we can take time to think of our loved ones and send them blessings through the divine. *We can be aware of our connection with the divine and the rest of the universe in any moment and at every moment.*

Staying connected with the divine is just a way to invite the most powerful and loving force in the universe to support and guide us. The divine is available 24 hours a day, 7 days a week. The only question is, "How often are we?"

60-Second Experience #21

- ➤ Bring to mind everything and everyone in your life you are thankful for.
- ➤ Notice all the ways the divine has already blessed you.
- ➤ Set an intention to connect with the divine, and invite the divine to guide you in this process.
- ➤ If you like, close your eyes.
- ➤ Silently breathe in and out for 30 seconds.
- ➤ **Ask the divine to help you know the best way to remind yourself of your connection.**
- ➤ **Declare that once you know this, you will do it as often as possible.**
- ➤ Be still, listen and receive any guidance that comes to you.
- ➤ Breathe in and out for 30 more seconds.
- ➤ Ask the divine to show you specifically how you can make this desire come true.
- ➤ Make a commitment to do what you need to do and be who you need to be in order to live the wisdom you receive.
- ➤ Thank the divine, and open your eyes.

Connecting without Offending Others

All of this connecting with the divine can be done in a way that does not lead other people to feel their rights are being violated. *When we're comfortable with our connection, we don't need to influence or change anyone. We are happy to be as we are. When we are truly connecting in a powerful way, our life will clearly show this. We will be so joyful, effective and confident that it will be obvious to everyone around us. People will seek us out and ask us to share our secret of fulfillment and enjoyment.*

It is not necessary for a man to shout out on the rooftops that he is a man. People can observe that without him saying a word. In fact, if someone has to convince us of something, we may want to look carefully at what's happening. For example, if someone goes out of his or her way to tell me how great of a friend they are and is constantly trying to persuade me to believe this, my first instinct is to wonder why all of this energy is spent on convincing me. It might feel like this person who is saying they are my friend might be trying to make me believe something that really isn't true.

A true friend doesn't need to convince us because his or her actions speak for themselves. A true follower of the divine doesn't have the need to say anything or persuade anyone. Such people know themselves, feel comfortable with their connection with the divine, and don't need others to agree or approve. The greatest spiritual teachers all share this quality.

60-Second Experience #22

> ➤ Bring to mind everything and everyone in your life you are thankful for.

> ➤ Notice all the ways the divine has already blessed you.

> ➤ Set an intention to connect with the divine, and invite the divine to guide you in this process.

> ➤ If you like, close your eyes.

> ➤ Silently breathe in and out for 30 seconds.

> ➤ **Declare to the divine that you wish to connect in the way that is best for you without making anyone else wrong.**

> ➤ **Ask the divine to remove any need to prove others are wrong or you are right.**

> ➤ Be still, listen and receive any guidance that comes to you.

> ➤ Breathe in and out for 30 more seconds.

> ➤ Ask the divine to show you specifically how you can make this desire come true.

> ➤ Make a commitment to do what you need to do and be who you need to be in order to live the wisdom you receive.

> ➤ Thank the divine, and open your eyes.

Asking for What You Want

Once you become comfortable connecting with the divine, you can begin asking specifically for whatever you want. The process becomes simpler as you use it more often.

All you need to do is follow the steps…

1) **_Become Aware_** *of all the ways the divine has blessed you in your life.*

2) **_Intend Connection_** *with the divine.*

3) **_Connect in Silence_**

4) **_Declare_** *what you wish to be, do or have.*

5) **_Ask_** *the divine to support you.*

6) **_Receive_** *wisdom from the divine.*

7) *Request and Get a **_Specific Action_** to help you apply the divine wisdom most effectively.*

8) **_Commit_** *to act and abandon ALL excuses.*

9) *Express your **_Gratitude_** to the divine.*

60-Second Experience #23

> ➤ Bring to mind everything and everyone in your life you are thankful for.
>
> ➤ Notice all the ways the divine has already blessed you.
>
> ➤ Set an intention to connect with the divine, and invite the divine to guide you in this process.
>
> ➤ If you like, close your eyes.
>
> ➤ Silently breathe in and out for 30 seconds.
>
> ➤ **Declare to the divine what you wish to be, do or have.**
>
> ➤ **Ask the divine to help you find the most effortless, loving and effective way to achieve this.**
>
> ➤ Be still, listen and receive any guidance that comes to you.
>
> ➤ Breathe in and out for 30 more seconds.
>
> ➤ Ask the divine to show you specifically how you can make this desire come true.
>
> ➤ Mae a commitment to do what you need to do and be who you need to be in order to live the wisdom you receive.
>
> ➤ Thank the divine.

Why It Works to Thank the Divine

Most have us have been told to thank the divine for all the blessings in our life, but we may have been told many different reasons why it is beneficial for us to do this. Some of the most common reasons for thanking the divine include the following:

- **Creation / Existence** – Because we would be nothing without the divine.

- **Divine Blessing** – We are truly blessed and we should be grateful.

- **Divine Approval** – If the divine likes us, we will be blessed.

- **Worship** – Because the divine is so great.

- **Divine Expectation** – The divine expects us to express our thanks.

- **Divine Abandonment** – The divine will leave us if we don't express appreciation.

- **Divine Repossession** – The divine will take back all our blessings if we are not thankful.

- **Divine Threat** – The divine will harm us if we do not express our gratitude.

The accuracy of many of these reasons is debatable, depending on each person's spiritual beliefs, and none of these reasons address one simple fact. ***Thanking the divine works!***

This may seem at first to be a very shallow reason to thank the divine, but it's not what most people think. This is not to say we can sweet talk the divine into giving us what we want – a practice which could be called divine flattery. Thanking the divine is simply a part of how the universe works. We ask, we receive, and we thank.

We ask because we need the help of the divine. We receive because of the generosity of the divine. We thank because (1) we are grateful, (2) it reminds us how generous the divine is, which (3) reminds us to ask again.

In this way we have an ongoing relationship with the divine. We have more than an "I'll call you when things get rough or when I need something" relationship. We have a two-way, continuous, flowing relationship.

For some, this may still feel like a relationship where we're asking for our allowance from our parents. This implies if we ask nicely, we'll get what we want because our parents can't defend themselves against our irresistible charms and puppy dog eyes.

It may serve us instead to think of the divine as an unconditionally loving and endlessly giving grandparent who has all their needs met and joyously shares their abundance with their grandchildren, who are loved so much.

Just like a grandchild who confidently and knowingly asks for abundance from her grandparents, we ask for what we want. We receive because the divine is generous, and we thank to renew the cycle.

It has been said that what distinguished the most powerful spiritual figures from others is that they knew, beyond a shadow of a doubt, that when they asked from the divine they would receive. When they did this, they always gave thanks.

60-Second Experience #24

- ➢ Bring to mind everything and everyone in your life you are thankful for.
- ➢ Notice all the ways the divine has already blessed you.
- ➢ Set an intention to connect with the divine, and invite the divine to guide you in this process.
- ➢ If you like, close your eyes.
- ➢ Silently breathe in and out for 30 seconds.
- ➢ **Thank the divine for all the blessings in your life, including the ones you're not aware of.**
- ➢ **Ask the divine to help you fully feel how blessed you are and help you maintain this attitude of gratitude.**
- ➢ Be still, listen and receive any guidance that comes to you.
- ➢ Breathe in and out for 30 more seconds.
- ➢ Make a commitment to do what you need to do and be who you need to be in order to live the wisdom you receive.
- ➢ Thank the divine and open your eyes.

The Opportunity to Serve

If there were no customers with unmet needs, there would be no work, no income, and no jobs. Most of us often forget why we are able to receive the money we do for our work. The simple reason we make money is that we're meeting a need someone else has. If there is no need, there will be no money.

So much of our experience at work is impacted by our view of our customers. *If we see customers or clients as demanding people who are bothering us in order to get what they want, we will probably experience work in an unpleasant way.* It will feel like "those people" are taking advantage of us, don't care about us, and are only looking out for themselves. When work is experienced this way, it can be extremely unfulfilling, annoying, and not fun.

When we see and understand that our life purpose is deeply connected to others in some way, we can reach the place of being where we look forward to serving others and fulfilling our mission. We realize that *work is simply a natural part of the cycle of giving and receiving. Sometimes we get to experience the wonderful feeling of receiving from others. This experience can validate our feelings of being someone who is worth receiving. At other times, we get to experience the magic feeling that comes from knowing we've helped another person meet their needs. This experience can help validate our feelings of doing work that is meaningful, valuable, and appreciated. With such an attitude, we experience joy on both sides of the giving and receiving cycle, and our life becomes a constant experience of joy – for we are always giving and receiving.*

Of course, the same cycle of giving and receiving can be experienced completely differently. We can complain about having to help someone else meet their needs, and we can complain that others aren't helping us meet our needs. In this way, our life becomes one big complaint because we experience frustration on both sides of the never-ending cycle.

The greatest spiritual teachers experienced enjoyment while giving and receiving. They demonstrated their understanding of the fact that it simply works to be joyful while giving and receiving.

It's not necessary to make a moral issue out of it or say that someone "should" give lovingly or else they're a "bad" person. Nobody needs to be labeled or made wrong. All we need to do is examine the lives of the most fulfilled beings to walk this planet, and we can find plenty of examples of lives lived joyfully in service of others.

When we decide to live our lives with such an attitude of joyful service, we get to experience the same joy and fulfillment that our greatest teachers did. We will then recognize that the only difference between them and us is that they did this most or all the time.

60-Second Experience #25

➤ Bring to mind everything and everyone in your life you are thankful for.

➤ Notice all the ways the divine has already blessed you.

➤ Set an intention to connect with the divine, and invite the divine to guide you in this process.

➤ If you like, close your eyes.

➤ Silently breathe in and out for 30 seconds.

➤ **Declare that you wish to bring an attitude of joyful and loving service to your work.**

➤ **Ask the divine to help you see and experience your work as an opportunity to serve.**

➤ Be still, listen and receive any guidance that comes to you.

➤ Breathe in and out for 30 more seconds.

➤ Make a commitment to do what you need to do and be who you need to be in order to live the wisdom you receive.

➤ Thank the divine and open your eyes.

Inspiration Breaks

The most powerful application of this work for me has been what could be called "Inspiration Breaks." Every hour, on the hour, while I'm working I take a break to connect with the divine. I just close my eyes, follow the process outlined in this book, and ask for whatever I need.

If I need energy, I ask for it, and I receive it. If I need inspiration, I ask for it, and I receive it. If I need an answer for something I'm working on, I ask for it, and I receive it. Whatever I need, I just ask, and I receive.

Inspiration breaks help me focus, relax, produce better, let go of stress, and do anything else I desire. The breathing slows my body and my mind down, and the divine fills me up with whatever I need.

When I don't take Inspiration Breaks, I feel rushed in my work. Stress gets the best of me, and I feel like I have to get everything done yesterday.

Inspiration Breaks are just one more way of inviting the divine into your everyday work life. They can be used inside and outside of work. They, like the divine, are powerful, nurturing, fulfilling, and loving.

Giving ourselves such nurturance demonstrates that we love and care for ourselves as much as the divine does. Most of us know how to be gentle and kind to ourselves, we just don't make the time to do so. It's as if we're saying we're not important enough or that others matter more than we do. When we give ourselves the gift of connecting with the divine, we allow ourselves to once again feel and experience the most divine part of our human nature. When we don't, we leave ourselves to experience only our human side.

The only question that remains is "What part or parts of us do we choose to experience?"

60-Second Experience #26

- ➢ Bring to mind everything and everyone in your life you are thankful for.
- ➢ Notice all the ways the divine has already blessed you.
- ➢ Set an intention to connect with the divine, and invite the divine to guide you in this process.
- ➢ If you like, close your eyes.
- ➢ Silently breathe in and out for 30 seconds.
- ➢ **Declare that you wish to experience the most divine part of yourself right now.**
- ➢ **Ask the divine to give you whatever you need in order to experience this right now.**
- ➢ Be still, listen and receive any guidance that comes to you.
- ➢ Breathe in and out for 30 more seconds.
- ➢ Make a commitment to do what you need to do and be who you need to be in order to live the wisdom you receive.
- ➢ Thank the divine and open your eyes.

The Hard Part

If it's so simple to connect with the divine, why don't we always do it? Why don't I always do it? The reasons may be similar to reasons why we don't exercise, eat in healthy ways, study for class, prepare properly for work, or meditate regularly.

Sometimes we might feel too tired to do it. Maybe we would rather do something else that seems more fun. Perhaps we resent the fact that it requires a constant and regular commitment, like exercise, and we'd rather have one big session and be done with it. There are many other reasons that all seem to fall under the same umbrella – we're human.

Why do we do things that work so well and then stop doing them? Maybe it's just human nature. We may never know why, but we can know one simple thing – it doesn't have to be difficult.

We don't have to make it complicated with justifications or rationalizations. We can simply recognize when we don't make the time to connect and commit again to connect in the very moment we become aware we've not maintained our connection.

We probably won't gain much by beating ourselves up, blaming others, or using other such tactics. None of these strategies have helped us exercise regularly or eat better, and it's unlikely they'll help us make a more regular connection with the divine.

There may be one additional obstacle to regularly connecting with the divine that may not exist in other areas of our life – guilt and shame. Some of us have been taught that the divine gets angry with us when we don't do things the way the divine wants. Others have been taught it is a sin to not maintain contact with the divine and that we must ask for forgiveness before we try to contact again.

These beliefs may or may not serve us. In order to best address them, it may serve us to connect with the divine and get our own answers from the divine. *We may wish to ask the divine if there's any reason we would ever not be welcome to communicate with the divine. The answer may surprise some of us.*

60-Second Experience #27

- ➢ Bring to mind everything and everyone in your life you are thankful for.
- ➢ Notice all the ways the divine has already blessed you.
- ➢ Set an intention to connect with the divine, and invite the divine to guide you in this process.
- ➢ If you like, close your eyes.
- ➢ Silently breathe in and out for 30 seconds.
- ➢ **Declare that you wish to make it easy for you to regularly connect with the divine.**
- ➢ **Ask the divine to help you do this.**
- ➢ Be still, listen and receive any guidance that comes to you.
- ➢ Breathe in and out for 30 more seconds.
- ➢ Make a commitment to do what you need to do and be who you need to be in order to live the wisdom you receive.
- ➢ Thank the divine and open your eyes.

Simple Transformation – Here and Now

Deciding to bring the divine into your everyday work life can be as simple as deciding to bring your lunch to work. It doesn't need to be dramatic, complicated, attention seeking, or anything difficult. Many people live their divine relationship very powerfully and quietly without telling others it is the source of their strength. Such people generally don't have the need to tell the whole world about it. They just live their divine connection simply, powerfully, and peacefully.

In fact, there are probably many people around you right now who quietly live a very spiritually connected life, both inside and outside of work. There may be one or many reasons why they don't discuss their divine relationship. Some people like to keep their relationship with the divine private, while others do so to respect others' desire not to hear about it. Some think work is not the place to discuss it, and others prefer to act rather than talk.

Every day, you have the option to connect with the most powerful force in the universe. You may ask this divine force to support you in you work, your relationships, your play, and everything in between. This all-knowing being has more knowledge and wisdom than any human or electronic business consultant, coach or expert you can find. The divine knows it all, and you can receive wisdom from the divine to help you align your professional life and activity with divine wisdom. ***You can do this today! You don't have to wait until tomorrow. You don't even have to wait 5 minutes. You can connect with the divine RIGHT NOW and begin***

receiving profoundly deep and powerful wisdom to guide you along your path.

You don't even have to go anywhere to connect with the divine. You don't need to be in a particular building or place. You don't have to work for a company that has spiritual principles at the core of its philosophy and operations (though you might eventually choose to do this). You don't have to work for a non-profit agency. You don't have to help the homeless or save the planet. (There are plenty of people right in front of you who need your help right now). You don't have to give a certain amount of your money to the poor, though you may choose to do so. *You don't have to do anything or go anywhere to open yourself up to receiving divine wisdom and guidance. You simply need to create time and get quiet enough to hear that still small voice inside you. If you can connect with that divinely inspired voice, and you commit to acting in the ways that you are divinely guided, there is no end to what is possible. With the divine, ALL THINGS ARE POSSIBLE! ALL THINGS!*

60-Second Experience #28

- ➢ Bring to mind everything and everyone in your life you are thankful for.
- ➢ Notice all the ways the divine has already blessed you.
- ➢ Set an intention to connect with the divine, and invite the divine to guide you in this process.
- ➢ If you like, close your eyes.
- ➢ Silently breathe in and out for 30 seconds.
- ➢ **Declare that you wish to begin living powerfully with your connections NOW.**
- ➢ **Ask the divine to help you open up to seeing what's possible for you if you commit to connecting on a regular basis.**
- ➢ Be still, listen and receive any guidance that comes to you.
- ➢ Breathe in and out for 30 more seconds.
- ➢ Make a commitment to do what you need to do and be who you need to be in order to live the wisdom you receive.
- ➢ Thank the divine and open your eyes.

What I'm Waiting For

I want to be a writer, but I don't know if anyone will read my books.

I want to be a teacher, but I have no students.

I want to be a healer, but I haven't got a degree.

I want to be a leader, but I don't know if anyone will follow me.

I want to do my work, but I don't know if I can make a living.

So I want and I wait, but nothing changes.

No external forces turn my wishes into realities.

No genie...no lamp...no magic.

Then...after a while...I wrote about the way I felt,
and I became a writer.

I shared this insight with my friend,
and I became a teacher.

I listened to my friend share her feelings,
and I became a healer.

Others saw that I did what I did without waiting for anyone's
permission,

And they did the same.
In that moment, I became a leader.

Finally, I realized that I was doing my work all along.
And I'm still alive

Acknowledgments

Thank you God... for everyone and everything in my life, especially Rossana. I am so blessed.

Thank you Dad, for showing me an example of a businessman I can be proud of and follow.

Thank you to all of the people whom I have worked with as clients for allowing me to practice this with you. Special thanks to those who have done coaching work with me. I have learned so much from who you are, and I have been constantly shown an example of what it's like for someone to live their highest values at work. Thank you to everyone at the Institute for Integrative Coaching by Debbie Ford. I have learned from your example a whole new understanding of what it means to be a person of service.

My intention is that all who read this, including myself, will experience the joy, bliss and fulfillment that come from connecting with the divine.

Love,

Wade

About the Author

Wade has led retreats and personal growth workshops, authored books on spirituality, personal growth, finance, parenting, business growth & more.

He has worked successfully as a life coach, 4-day work week mentor, organizational consultant, computer trainer, sales consultant, executive coach, speaker, mental health counselor, management consultant, software designer and programmer, author, business analyst, financial counselor, and in many other capacities.

Wade has a Bachelor's degree in Marketing and a Master's degree in Mental Health Counseling Psychology.

He lives happily with his wife and children.

His email address is wade@wadegalt.com .

Author Blog & Website

You may visit Wade's blog & website at www.wadegalt.com .

Get the Workbook & Journal for Free

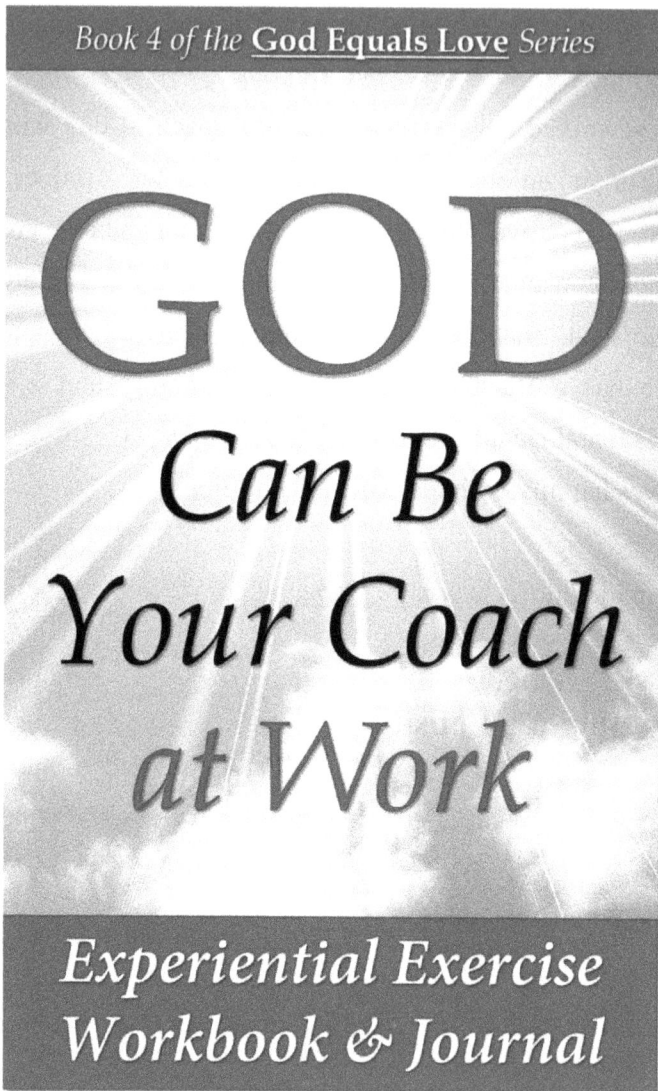

Book 4 of the **God Equals Love** Series

GOD
Can Be
Your Coach
at Work

Experiential Exercise
Workbook & Journal

Get the exercises from this book in printable (PDF) format
so you can type or write them out and track your progress.

Go to www.wadegalt.com/godcoachworkjournal

Also by Wade Galt

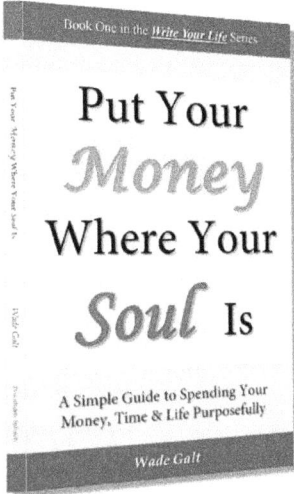

Book One in the *Write Your Life* Series

Put Your Money Where Your Soul Is

A Simple Guide to Spending Your
Money, Time and Life Purposefully

Learn how to free up additional time, money and energy by redefining your relationships with money, time, people, and things.

Simple strategies, exercises & tools help you make powerful changes with very little effort or struggle.

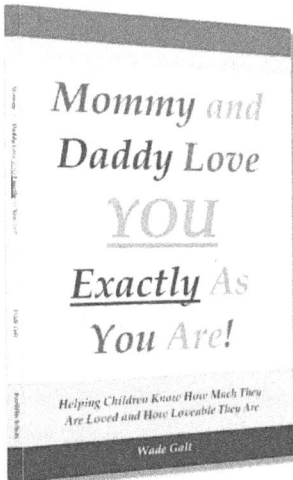

Mommy and Daddy Love You Exactly As You Are!

Helping Children Know How Much They
Are Loved and How Loveable They Are

My hope is that this book helps you...

1) Let your child or children know how special they are.

2) Remember how special your child or children are.

3) Understand how much your parents love(d) you, whether or not they ever shared this with you.

Mommy Loves You Exactly As You Are!

Helping Children Know How Much They Are Loved and How Loveable They Are

My hope is that this book helps you...

1) Let your child or children know how special they are.

2) Remember how special your child or children are.

3) Understand how much your parents love(d) you, whether or not they ever shared this with you.

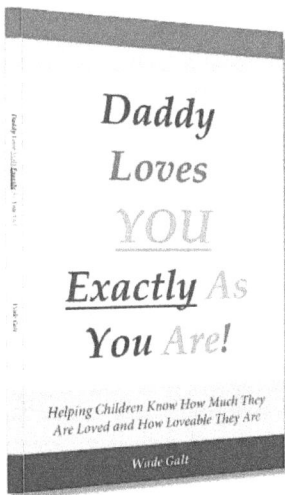

Daddy Loves You Exactly As You Are!

Helping Children Know How Much They Are Loved and How Loveable They Are

My hope is that this book helps you...

1) Let your child or children know how special they are.

2) Remember how special your child or children are.

3) Understand how much your parents love(d) you, whether or not they ever shared this with you.

The *God Equals Love* Book Series

(Free eBook Versions Available for All Books)

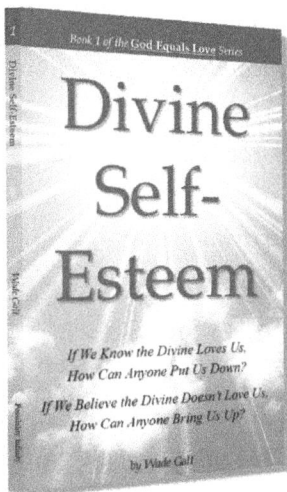

Book 1 - Divine Self-Esteem

Learning to Love Ourselves
the Way the Divine Loves Us

If we know the Divine loves us, how can anyone put us down?

If we believe the Divine doesn't love us, how can anyone bring us up?

Learn to see yourself through divinely loving eyes and catch a glimpse of the divinely-made miracle you are.

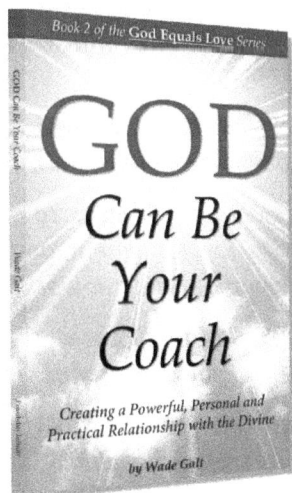

Book 2 - GOD Can Be Your Coach

Creating a Powerful, Personal and
Practical Relationship with the Divine

Create More Joy, Happiness, Love, Peace and Purpose in Your Life.

Learn One Simple Way to form a more powerful connection & relationship.

If You Knew You Could Connect with the Divine Anytime You Choose to Receive Guidance, Support, and Peace, Would You?

Will You?

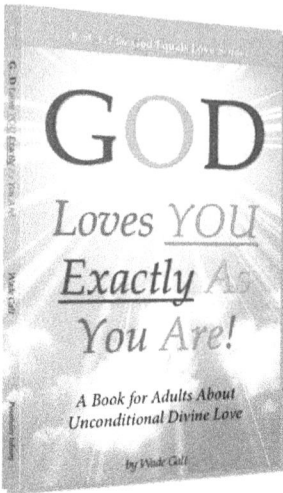

3 - GOD Loves You Exactly As You Are!

Understanding & Experiencing
Unconditional Divine Love

An Invitation to Consider & Experience the Life-Altering Understanding That You are Completely and Unconditionally Loved and Loveable EXACTLY AS YOU ARE!

What If God Loves You EXACTLY as You are?

How Would Understanding that Transform Your Life?

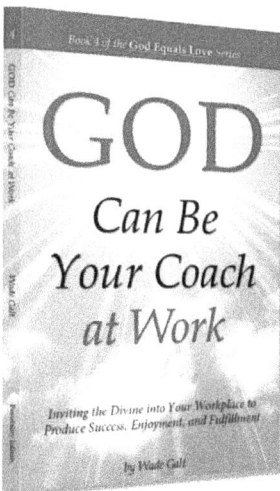

Book 4 - GOD Can Be Your Coach at Work

Inviting the Divine into Your Workplace to Produce Success, Enjoyment & Fulfillment

Few of us fully live our highest spiritual values in our workplace.

This is a source of frustration, shame, guilt & dissatisfaction for billions of us.

What if the divine actually wants us to experience life, love, joy, fulfillment, and abundance inside and outside our work?

What if the divine cares about our work simply because the divine cares for us?

This book is an invitation to work WITH the divine to create divinely inspired results for you and the world.

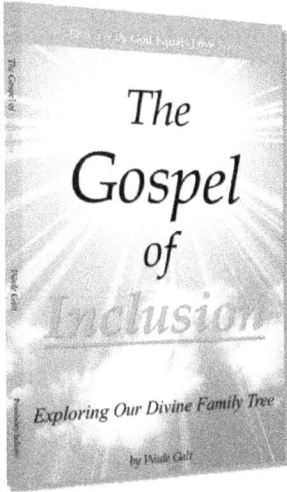

Book 5 - The Gospel of Inclusion

Exploring Our Divine Family Tree

Who is included in God's plan? Is it only people like me? Only people like you? What atrocities & apathy do we justify daily by declaring others are outside of God's chosen circle of people?

What if we really are part of one divine family? What would that mean? How would we have to change?

WARNING! Reading this book may lead you to (1) consider the possibility that we're all God's children and (2) do something about that. Proceed at your own risk!

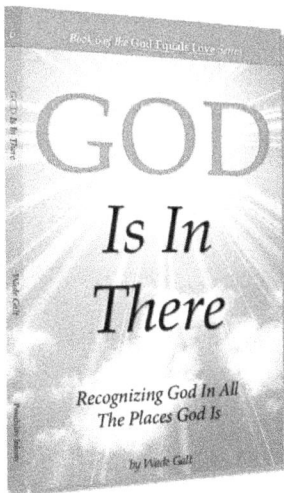

Book 6 - God Is In There

Recognizing God In All The Places God Is

If you could teach only one spiritual lesson, what would you teach?

What truth could you share that is so powerful, it would fundamentally transform the way others live?

There are a few core ideas that most spiritual traditions hold as true. Some believe that the most powerful and life-transforming truths are so self-evident and so obvious that all traditions agree about them.

This book contains one of those ideas.

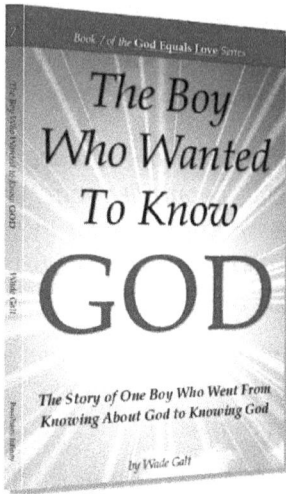

7 - The Boy Who Wanted to Know God

The Story of One Boy Who Went from Knowing About God to Knowing God

What would you be willing to do in order to meet God?

Join a curious and excited young boy on his journey to meeting the divine.

You might meet God, too.

The journey may be shorter and simpler than you think.

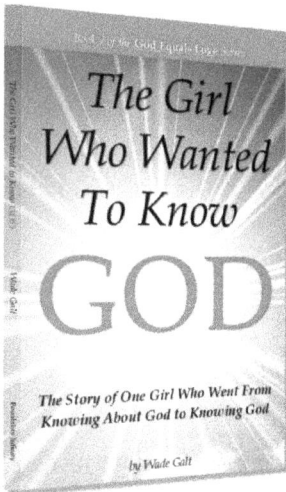

7 - The Girl Who Wanted to Know God

The Story of One Girl Who Went from Knowing About God to Knowing God

What would you be willing to do in order to meet God?

Join a curious and excited young girl on her journey to meeting the divine.

You might meet God, too.

The journey may be shorter and simpler than you think.

Translated into Spanish (More to Come)

Autoestima Divina

Aprendiendo a Amarnos De la Forma en que Dios nos Ama

Si sabemos que el Divino nos ama, ¿cómo podemos sentirnos mal con nosotros mismos?

Si creemos que el Divino no nos ama, ¿cómo podemos sentirnos bien con nosotros mismos?

Aprender a verse a sí mismo a través de los ojos de amor de Dios y echar un vistazo a el milagro hecho de Dios-que eres.

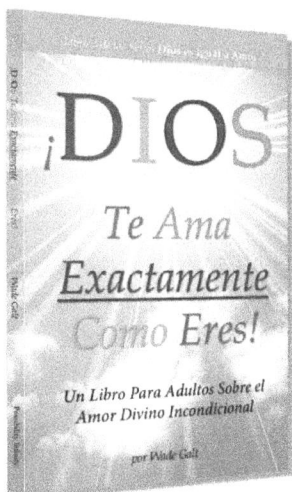

DIOS Te Ama Exactamente Como Eres

Un Libro Para Adultos Sobre el Amor Divino Incondicional

¿Y Si Dios te ama EXACTAMENTE como eres? ¿De que manera ese entendimiento transformaría tu vida?

Esto Es Una Simple Invitación... Para Considerar y Experimentar... Un Entendimiento de la Vida Alternativo...

Tú Eres Completa e Incondicionalmente... Amado y Adorable... EXACTAMENTE COMO ERES!

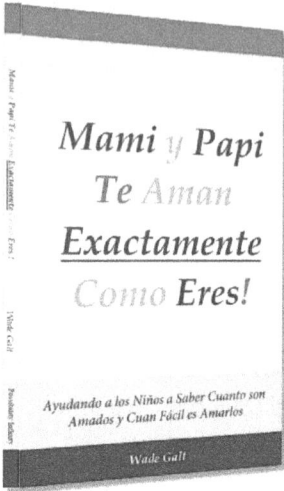

Mami y Papi Te Aman Exactamente Como Eres!

Ayudando a los Niños a Saber Cuanto son Amados y Cuan Fácil es Amarlos

Mi esperanza es que este libro te ayude a...

1) Hacer que tus niños sepan cuan especiales son.

2) Recordarte cuan especiales son tus niños.

3) Comprender cuanto te aman o te amaron tus padres ya sea que compartieran o no esto contigo.

Mami Te Ama Exactamente Como Eres!

Ayudando a los Niños a Saber Cuanto son Amados y Cuan Fácil es Amarlos

Mi esperanza es que este libro te ayude a...

1) Hacer que tus niños sepan cuan especiales son.

2) Recordarte cuan especiales son tus niños.

3) Comprender cuanto te aman o te amaron tus padres ya sea que compartieran o no esto contigo.

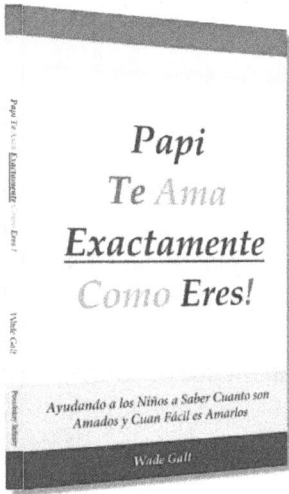

Papi Te Ama Exactamente Como Eres!

Papi Te Ama Exactamente Como Eres!

Ayudando a los Niños a Saber Cuanto son Amados y Cuan Fácil es Amarlos

Mi esperanza es que este libro te ayude a...

1) Hacer que tus niños sepan cuan especiales son.

2) Recordarte cuan especiales son tus niños.

3) Comprender cuanto te aman o te amaron tus padres ya sea que compartieran o no esto contigo.

To see these books and other books not listed here, visit www.wadegalt.com/books .

All profits from the sale of the GOD EQUALS LOVE books go to organizations and charities that seek to end unnecessary hunger and poverty.

New Book & Program Notifications

If you'd like to be emailed when we release new books, audios and other programs please visit www.wadegalt.com/notifiy to sign up for these notifications.

Share the Message & the Love

I hope this helps you see & feel how truly amazing and miraculous of a creation you are and how much the divine values you.

If you found the book to be helpful, would you please be so kind as to write a review on Amazon for the book or share the book on Facebook, Instagram, Twitter or other social media so others may know how it helped you?

Even if it's a super-short review, every little bit helps.

Thank you so much.

If there's anything I can do to help you further with this work, please email me at is wade@wadegalt.com .

All my best,

Wade

www.ingramcontent.com/pod-product-compliance
Lightning Source LLC
Chambersburg PA
CBHW061148040426
42445CB00013B/1609